David Darst

More Praise for

The Little Book
That Saves Your Assets

". . . insightful, tidy, essential, provocative, and witty . . ."

Jerry Goodman, a.k.a Adam Smith,
Author of *The Money Game* and *Supermoney*

"All too often, wisdom arrives in heavy doses. But not with David Darst. Although the wisdom he provides has extraordinary value, Darst delivers it here like fine champagne: full of sparkle and so good you hate to finish it. All investors have much to gain from his sparkling advice."

Peter L. Bernstein, Author of *Capital Ideas, Against the Gods, The Power of Gold,* and *Capital Ideas Evolving*

"Asset allocation is an art, David Darst is the master. Now he has put it into an entertaining and readable form that enables individual investors to do what the pros do, build and save their assets!"

Consuelo Mack, Anchor and Managing Editor, *Consuelo Mack WealthTrack* on PBS.

THE LITTLE BOOK

THAT
SAVES
YOUR
ASSETS

Little Book Big Profits Series

In the *Little Book Big Profits* series, the brightest icons in the financial world hold forth on topics ranging from tried-and-true investment strategies to tomorrow's new trends. Each book offers a unique perspective on investing, allowing the reader to pick and choose from the very best in investment advice today.

Books in the *Little Book Big Profits* series include:

The Little Book That Beats the Market, where Joel Greenblatt, founder and managing partner at Gotham Capital, reveals a "magic formula" that is easy to use and makes buying good companies at bargain prices automatic, enabling you to successfully beat the market and professional managers by a wide margin.

The Little Book of Value Investing, where Christopher Browne, managing director of Tweedy, Browne Company, LLC, the oldest value investing firm on Wall Street, simply and succinctly explains how value investing, one of the most effective investment strategies ever created, works, and shows you how it can be applied globally.

The Little Book of Common Sense Investing, where Vanguard Group Founder John C. Bogle shares his own time-tested philosophies, lessons, and personal anecdotes to explain why outperforming the market is an investor illusion, and how the simplest of investment strategies—indexing—can deliver the greatest return to the greatest number of investors.

The Little Book That Makes You Rich, where Louis Navellier, financial analyst and editor of investment newsletters since 1980, offers readers a fundamental understanding of how to get rich using the best in growth investing strategies. Filled with in-depth insights and practical advice, *The Little Book That Makes You Rich* outlines an effective approach to building true wealth in today's markets.

The Little Book That Builds Wealth, where Pat Dorsey, director of stock analysis for leading independent investment research provider Morningstar, Inc., guides the reader in understanding "economic moats," learning how to measure them against one another, and selecting the best companies for the very best returns.

The Little Book That Saves Your Assets, where David Darst, a managing director of Morgan Stanley who chairs the firm's Global Wealth Management Asset Allocation and Investment Policy Committee, explains the role of asset allocation in maximizing investment returns to meet life objectives. Brimming with the wisdom gained from years of practical experience, this book is a vital road map to a secure financial future.

THE LITTLE BOOK

THAT

SAVES

YOUR

ASSETS

What the Rich Do to Stay Wealthy

in Up and Down Markets

DAVID M. DARST

FOREWORD BY JAMES J. CRAMER

WILEY

John Wiley & Sons, Inc.

Published by John Wiley & Sons, Inc., Hoboken, New Jersey.
Published simultaneously in Canada.

For general information on our other products and services or for technical support, please contact our
Customer Care Department within the United States at (800) 762-2974, outside the United States at
(317) 572-3993 or fax (317) 572-4002.

Wiley also publishes its books in a variety of electronic formats. Some content that appears in print
may not be available in electronic books. For more information about Wiley products, visit our web site
at www.wiley.com.

Library of Congress Cataloging-in-Publication Data:

Darst, David M.
    The little book that saves your assets: what the rich do to stay wealthy in up and down markets /
David M. Darst.
      p. cm.—(Little book big profits series)
    Includes bibliographical references.
    ISBN 978-0-470-25004-4 (cltoh)
      1. Portfolio management.   2. Investments. I. Title.
    HG4529.5.D372   2008
    332.6—dc22

                                          2008014639

Printed in the United States of America

10 9 8 7 6

For
Guy, Susan, and Jim,
Bob, Eleanor, and Kim,
Diane, Elizabeth, David, and Charlie

Contents

Foreword

~

I would tell you that David Darst is one of the best investors out there, but that doesn't do him justice. The man is a financial visionary, an incredible teacher, and knowledgeable beyond belief. Let me put it this way: David has figured out more markets than I have ever traded in. He has been *the* dominant thinker when it comes to the vast panoply of investments out there. He's your guide through the financial supermarket we must all navigate, and without him, you will most surely get lost in the myriad aisles and end up buying the wrong thing at the wrong time. And in this supermarket there is no money-back guarantee. Or, to switch metaphors, with so many new things you can invest in, picking the right ones has become as difficult and frightening as climbing Mount Everest without this Sherpa showing you the way.

So I thought I was prepared when I started reading *The Little Book That Saves Your Assets*. I'd read David's earlier books and loved them, especially *The Art of Asset Allocation*, a guidebook that professionals thumb through when they get stumped. And when I first worked with David at Goldman Sachs, I cut my teeth on his *Complete Bond Book*, which I still consider the best treatment of the subject yet written. Until I devoured it I thought I knew how the stock market worked; silly me. David explained that the bond market is the fundament that everything else gets priced off of. That bit of advice makes the difference between amateurs and professionals, and they don't teach it anywhere. *The Art of Asset Allocation* remains on my *Mad Money* desk, right next to my terminals that flicker stock prices, a permanent warning that I am being foolish if I think only of individual stocks and not a caller's broader array of life savings.

But this book is something else entirely: the most accessible guide I've ever seen to applying the most fundamental principle of investing, asset allocation. Asset allocation, not stock picking, not sector funds, not guessing the direction of the Dow Jones averages, is the key to financial success. This book should be required reading for every nonprofessional investor, not to mention many of the pros who still don't get it. In fact, even if you have no desire to manage your own money, you should still read this book, because David has strategies in here that can work for everyone who wants to grow wealth or simply protect it. This book is pretty much a one-decision guide—either you want to lose your assets or you want to save them; the former group shouldn't bother with what Darst has to say, while the latter group needs it *now*!

We've been flooded with books that promise to do just that, books that often either aren't worth reading or are unreadable. *The Little Book That Saves Your Assets* is just the opposite. Why? In part it's because David is a stellar teacher. I know this firsthand because he was my first real teacher at Goldman Sachs, and it's hard not to mention another of David's former protégés, Eddie Lampert, a phenomenal hedge fund manager with a great track record, whom David recruited as a teenager right out of high school. Back then he taught us poetry and literature while he drilled us over and over again on the basics. Decades later he's still got the knack, working Yeats and Robert Frost into his advice and explanations. Investing for English majors—sounds good to me. He makes it enjoyable, he makes the necessary *fun*!

David also knows how to put his metaphors to work, and that matters more than you might expect. On Wall Street the pros use complicated-sounding language to refer to concepts that aren't that hard to understand when someone explains them in plain English. But a lot of the pros would rather make you feel confused and dependent on their services, rather than educating you. Time and again David takes complex or arcane-sounding terms and translates them into easy-to-understand football metaphors. This book will do more than educate you; it will empower you as an investor. For example, David has a great section on how to rigorously determine if a fund manager is any good that's downright aggressive. Most wouldn't dare to invade that territory. David has pioneered it, has mapped it, and knows who is out of bounds, who's off the reservation. Can you assess a fund manager without him? I think not.

There's a lot of great advice in here, but the reason you can't afford not to read this book boils down to this: Smart asset allocation, which includes diversification (a necessity I address endlessly on my TV show *Mad Money*), is the single best way to avoid losing lots of money. Even if you think you have these concepts nailed down, believe me, there's always more to learn, and David Darst, the man who taught me everything I know about the subject, is the man to teach you. Until this book, I thought that you had to work at Goldman for so many years, or at Morgan Stanley, where he's the asset allocator himself, to get this sage's advice. Not any more. He's made the basics come alive, and with this book you can be sure that your chances of being a big-time client of David's firm increase dramatically.

I am proud of my three-decade-long-association with David, but even more proud to call this asset allocation icon my friend. Read this book, learn what he has to say, and you will be richer for it in more ways than having more money, as I have been since the day I met him as a young aspiring job-seeker at Goldman Sachs so many years ago. You've picked the right book. I wish he had written it 30 years ago, but it's never too late for a new classic to appear on the financial literary scene.

—Jim Cramer
Columnist for The Street.com
Columnist for *New York* magazine
Host of CNBC's *Mad Money*

Introduction

<hr/>

Just after we entered the New Millennium in 2000, I was asked to give investment advice to the 30-year-old founder and CEO of a high-flying dotcom company (from their ads, you would know the name, but it's gone now!) and his 50-year-old accountant and Chief Financial Officer. The high-tech CEO refused to heed my pleadings to transform *at least some* of his holdings into a diversified asset allocation plan, telling me, "My $2 billion net worth is going to become $10 billion, just you watch!"

By contrast, his accountant/CFO, who had *one-fiftieth* as much stock in the dotcom company as the CEO, listened thoughtfully to my summation of the importance of asset allocation and replied, "We *have* to allocate all this money into an appropriate mix of U.S. and non-U.S. stocks, bonds, real estate, commodities, hedge funds, inflation-protected securities, and cash. I want to hang on to this windfall and make it grow over time. There's *no way* an accountant like me right now should be worth tens of millions of dollars!"

You guessed it. After the crash and meltdown in the tech stocks, the Icarus-like CEO's golden wings melted and he plunged to earth, and his asset-allocating former accountant/CFO is now worth much more than he is.

Why is this so? In short, asset allocation. In *The Little Book that Saves Your Assets* I will introduce you to the techniques the rich use to stay wealthy in both up and down markets.

For centuries, fortunes have been made, preserved, or lost because people either paid careful attention to, or ignored, the main tenets of asset allocation. From Joseph in the Old Testament, through the Greeks, the Romans, the Venetians, the Spanish, and others, to the great banking fortunes of the Barings and the Rothschilds, and up to the Modern Era—Astor, Rockefeller, Carnegie, DuPont, and now Gates and Buffett, money has been compounded, accumulated, and *retained* by following the key ideas of asset allocation: diversification, rebalancing, risk management, and reinvestment. By the same token, mighty empires have fallen and fortunes have withered away when families and nations have let themselves get too concentrated in one kind of asset and thus far too exposed to risk.

Asset allocation, which also encompasses portfolio rebalancing, loss control, and the careful selection of investment managers, has been the driving force behind the growth and preservation of wealth in the endowments of Harvard, Yale, Princeton, Notre Dame, the University of Texas, Stanford, and many other universities, foundations, and large family fortunes.

For generations, asset allocation has helped build wealth, protect wealth, and extend wealth. And now, owing to broader access to information via the Internet, to innovative and low-cost financial instruments such as exchange-traded funds, and to user-friendly software and portfolio optimization tools, everyone can practice what was once only the domain of the wealthy and the sophisticated. And this is not only a nice thing to have, it has become critically important to tens of millions of individual investors who have had the burden of investment responsibility shifted from a defined benefit/guaranteed pension plan *onto their own shoulders* in the form of the IRA and 401(k) plans that they personally are responsible for.

In pro football, they say that "Offense wins games, Defense wins championships, and Special Teams win the Super Bowl." Asset allocation is the package of all these disciplines: (i) making money; (ii) not losing money; (iii) and rebalancing the asset mix when things get out of line and overconcentrated.

A few years ago, a securities broker introduced me to a young couple who while dating were sitting on the couch at her parents' home when they looked up at the television set to learn they had just won the State Lottery: Lots of money! Several brokerage firms and investment managers told them to put most of the cash into residential real estate and homebuilders stocks, since home prices then (in 2004 and 2005) were rising nationwide at almost 15 percent per year.

I told them no way! To do asset allocation right requires five easy steps. First, try to know yourself, your biases, your strengths and failings, your mental makeup and psychology. Second, decide whether you are really able to do-it-yourself or whether you should hire others. Some of us have the skills to fix a leaky sink, and others will only make it worse. Third, have a framework (this book supplies one, in Chapter 11) to critically evaluate the resources that you will use yourself, or that you will employ. Fourth, get input from a trusted, impartial, and caring source of life-wisdom and financial insight. (This person is your Uncle Frank, who you will meet in Chapter 2 and hear from throughout this book.) Fifth, make a plan and force yourself to revisit it from time to time.

Oh, by the way. The young couple got married, in a highly publicized yet classy and dignified ceremony, and rather than putting most of their eggs into the residential real estate basket, they judiciously spread out their assets over a mix of U.S. and non-U.S. assets and investment management styles. I'm happy to report that their lives, their portfolio, and their family are thriving.

When you turn on the television, read blog postings on the web, or visit the business section of a bookstore, you will notice that most of the financial experts are pushing their own personal route to riches—commodities, small-cap stocks, hedge funds, gold mining shares, you name it. Asset allocation helps you judge, balance, and blend many different types of investments and managers, depending on your personal circumstances, your market outlook, and the state of the world.

There is no magic formula for success in asset allocation. As with any human endeavor that has a lot of art in it, patience, perspective, curiosity, and emotional intelligence should be your steadfast allies. You should cultivate them and keep them close. Like a tailor-made suit, in asset allocation you use the same fabric as everyone else, but your fit will be different and yours individually.

Why You Need Asset Allocation

Simply stated, you need asset allocation for three main reasons. First, by diversifying your investments among several asset classes so that some are thriving regardless of the economic and financial environment, asset allocation helps you create and grow wealth. Second, by focusing on portfolio protection and risk as well as on return, asset allocation can help mitigate losses and contain the risks of an investment. Third, by inciting you with some degree of regularity to face reality, take action, and rebalance to your long-term weightings, asset allocation begets mental fortification and psychological stability.

Asset allocation represents a means of making your investment money work *for you,* instead of working *on you.* Asset allocation is grounded in flexibility, realism, preparedness, and self-knowledge. Asset allocation prevents you from becoming dogmatically wedded to a small number of asset classes or investment approaches, which do well for a certain period of time and then languish—whether they be commodities, real estate, cash, junk bonds, option strategies, emerging market stocks, or large-cap U.S. growth companies. Asset allocation relies on such tools as diversification, the tendency of assets to even out their performance over time, rebalancing, and pure common sense to take advantage of the normal cycles of life as well as the occasional periods of euphoria and despair, which have occurred sporadically in markets of every type throughout recorded history.

To sum up, asset allocation is the sine qua non of long-term investment success, and success in asset allocation requires:

- Facing yourself (you'll learn how in Chapter 6);
- Selecting someone who likes and knows you, your dreams, hopes, fears, biases, and addictions (Your Uncle Frank, who enters the scene in Chapter 2 and whose presence permeates this book); and
- Choosing people who know markets, have perspective, and understand investment value (We'll show you how to do this in Chapter 11).

Godspeed and Excelsior.

We All Do It (Even if We Don't Realize It)

Don't Let Your Plan Be an Accident

IN AN EPISODE FROM THE hit television series *The Sopranos*, Tony Soprano asked his wife to let him bet her real estate earnings on what he thinks is a surefire gamble. When she asks why he doesn't use the bundles of cash he has squirreled away over the years, Tony tells her that his cash is for emergencies and that all his other assets are tied up in what he calls *asset allocation*. Whether aware of it or not, we all have an asset allocation plan—even HBO drama characters. What I hope to do in this book is show you how to allocate your assets in such a way that you can meet your goals in a manner consistent with your personality.

Let's first understand what asset allocation is and how it has evolved over the years. When I was first exposed to the concept back in the 1980s, asset allocation was pretty much limited to international assets. Japan and Europe in particular were coming into their own as legitimate financial markets and were behaving in a completely different way from the U.S. markets. China had opened up to the world, and Japan was well on the rise. In the United States, we were using non–U.S. stocks, bonds, and cash to help us achieve higher returns and stay diversified to avoid being totally dependent on a few investments to achieve our goals.

In the 1990s, the field of asset allocation began to broaden. New research was being developed, and we began to look at markets and portfolios differently. Instead of just buying a mutual fund and considering ourselves diversified, we began to look at the investment world in categories such as large cap or small cap. We looked at managers' styles as being either growth or value, and we sought a balance of styles and capitalizations in our portfolio. As the decade progressed, manager and style selection became important tools to diversify investment portfolios.

By the late 1990s, a most curious thing began to unfold in the investment world. As the Internet and telecommunications became faster and more efficient, the world became much smaller. Much of the point of asset allocation is to find assets that not only can grow, but that behave in a manner different from other assets in the portfolio. When something is declining in price because of financial and economic events, it is nice to have something in the portfolio that is going up in price because of the same events. We call this *noncorrelation* and as you will see throughout the book, it is an important part of proper asset allocation. In the 1980s and early 1990s, you could generally achieve this by owning international stocks and bonds. Stocks in Japan tended to react primarily to Japanese events. European stocks were influenced by European news and generally moved differently from U.S. stocks. However, the approach of the New Millennium ushered in an increasingly global economy. Many of the same macro policies and factors that affected Ford also affected BMW and Toyota. Previously, all the fish swam in their own individual directions. As the planet shrank, the fish became a school and tended to swim together in the same way.

As we moved into the twenty-first century, new tools were created to meet investors' needs for assets that would act differently from each other. Portfolios began to include new asset classes such as gold, commodities, real estate investment trusts, inflation-protected securities, and certain types of hedge funds, which became important tools to generate returns that were not related to the same events. We began looking at different styles of money management. Rather than just buying stocks and bonds, we looked at strategies such as merger arbitrage and short selling to round out portfolios and achieve the results we were hoping for.

At its heart, the essence of asset allocation is the search for noncorrelation. Let's put it in football terms. To win at investing, we need to have a balanced team. We need to have parts of our portfolio that play great offense when times are good. We need defensive investments that are ferocious protectors of our territory when the economy is out of whack and things are not so great. Just as a good football team needs a good kicker to get points after touchdowns and kick field goals, we need some investments that provide steady excess returns regardless of economic conditions. To win, we have to be good at all aspects of the game. A sound asset allocation plan is how we build our team.

Just as a football team starts by evaluating players in the draft, to develop a plan we need to put together an organized current and projected view of you, your goals, your financial circumstances, and importantly, your behavioral and personality quirks. We have to have a general sense of what certain kinds of assets (such as stocks, bonds, cash, commodities, or real estate) can and cannot do for you. Once we have an idea of what we are working with and each player's talents and abilities, we need to develop and follow a game plan. We have to develop a portfolio of diversified investments so that some of our assets tend to be doing well when other assets tend to be languishing. Once the game is under way, we need to look at the portfolio from time to time to see whether we should cut back on investments that have exhibited rapid growth or judiciously add to other sound investments that have temporarily declined in value. A good football coach is always looking at the whole field and paying attention to what can go wrong. So should we. We always need to be thinking about how various kinds of risks can affect our assets, so we can take steps to reduce or offset such risks.

In many ways, investors today are fortunate. In the past 10 years, I have seen an explosion in investment products and investment information sources. Now it is possible for all investors to use the tools that were once available only to institutions such as retirement funds, endowments, and the very wealthy. Financially oriented television and radio programs; Internet-based web sites and blogs; and abundant articles, books, and brochures provide objective (and sometimes, not so objective) education and advice about investing. New financial instruments such as open-end and closed-end mutual funds, exchange-traded funds (ETFs), and depositary receipts have made it much easier for everyone to access all kinds of asset classes. These range from small- and mid-cap domestic stocks to international stocks and bonds, to gold, silver, inflation-protected securities, and specialized investment strategies such as those that focus on specific industry sectors that profit when prices fall.

The good news is that everyone has an all-access backstage pass to just about every type of investment, investment strategy, and risk management scheme there is. A brave new world of investment opportunity sits right outside your door (or inside the computer sitting on your desk), and you can put it to great use in growing your wealth, just as savvy and wealthy investors have for generations. First and foremost, you will have to decide if you are a do-it-yourselfer or if you prefer to bring in the pros. You may be brilliant at picking specific stocks, but have absolutely no interest in thinking about your overall portfolio, future planning, or risk management. Conversely, you may have no interest in picking stocks, and bonds may bore you, but you may love thinking about the big moves of asset allocation.

Putting together a game plan involves deciding what you need each player to do for the team. Likewise, proper asset allocation involves knowing what you want your assets to do for you. Are you at a stage in your life (and in a frame of mind) where it is more important to increase your wealth? For instance, if you are young and saving for college or for a newborn child, the money saved won't be used for quite some time, and what those future tuition bills will look like could be anyone's guess. The young parent will likely need a lot of money nearly 20 years in the future, and so these funds can be marked for aggressive capital growth, which may put them all in stocks. Stocks tend to be volatile and may swing wildly with short-term price declines and losses, but over time have tended to provide the highest return. However, if you are saving to buy a house in three years, you might not be willing to suffer any short-term losses. Therefore these funds will demand a different strategy, because you will want to protect the principal value.

Think of your money as the players on your team. You want quarterbacks to throw the ball accurately and tackles to block. Some of the most disappointed investors I've seen over the years had perfectly good investments; the problem was that they didn't allocate their investments according to their needs, and so their returns suffered. Monies had to be pulled from stock funds before they experienced great appreciation; perfectly good bond funds were used improperly as long-term investments; and money market accounts were incorrectly used as retirement savings. It's not enough to pick great investments— you have to pick the best investments for the right reasons.

We have our game plan. We know what we need each player to do. Now we have to look at what kind of field conditions we have, and what the weather will be like come game time. If we have a game plan built around throwing the ball and it's raining with 20-mile-an-hour winds, we are going to need to make some adjustments to the plan. It is the same with our investments; we need to think about what type of economic, financial, political, and geopolitical environment we are likely to face. Of course, even economists disagree, and predictions for the future vary widely, but you do need to have a sense of where things might be going. Are the domestic and global economies expected to be in a period of progress, stagnation, or decline? Are the financial markets favorably positioned for investment, or are they undergoing an era of turmoil, turbulence, and high volatility? Are prevailing political trends (such as taxes, regulation, and public opinion) investor-friendly or unfriendly? Are nations and regions behaving toward one another in a cooperative way, or in a confrontational way? All these background conditions can affect your asset allocation decisions toward or away from stocks, bonds, cash, or other kinds of assets.

If you are playing offense and investing somewhat assertively or aggressively to take advantage of a favorable economic environment, you may have certain kinds of players on the field, such as domestic and international stocks. On the other hand, if you are playing defense, your players may be heavily weighted toward high-grade bonds, cash, and perhaps inflation-protected securities. Which players you use will be determined by your investment temperament, outlook, and personal circumstances. Picking the best investments is important, but we live in a world where you can't just pick and be done with it. We inhabit a fast-changing world and global economy today. You need to reevaluate and rotate players in and out of the portfolio as the financial outlook changes, as your investments increase or decrease in value, and as your own monetary and personal situation changes over time.

One of the most fundamental elements of asset allocation is diversification. In my mind this is one of the most overused and least understood words in all of investing. True diversification involves having several distinct kinds of asset classes that perform differently from each other in different kinds of financial environments. For example, some investments, such as commodities and precious metals, may thrive in a high inflation environment while other assets, such as government bonds, tend to excel in a strongly disinflationary or deflationary environment. Depending on the financial outlook and the investor's mindset, it generally makes sense to have exposure to at least a few and perhaps several asset classes. I've seen too many investors make the mistake of thinking that they have a diversified portfolio when in fact they own nothing more than a list of assets that all go up or down in price together. I counseled a gentleman who thought he had a diversified portfolio because he owned dozens of stocks. When I reviewed the list, I found that he had a great many airline and trucking stocks. He owned different types of passenger airlines and also delivery companies like Federal Express. He had read that having a large number of stocks was how you diversified a portfolio. His background was in the transportation industry and he thought the economy would do well, so he included the trucking and shipping companies. Guess what? This portfolio is totally nondiversified. The same economic events will affect just about every stock he owns in the same way. Rising oil prices would be negative for his entire portfolio. As I meet with investors and talk to financial advisors around the world, I find this approach all too common. I meet investors who own six different mutual funds and think they are diversified. If they are the large popular funds, the investors probably own many of the same stocks in each fund, and all of the funds will react the same way to the same events. In the late 1990s, fund after fund owned virtually the same Internet and technology stocks. It didn't matter how many funds investors bought, they were just increasing their exposure to the dotcom bubble, not truly diversifying.

Diversification will not only make your portfolio less volatile, it will also make your reaction to the state of the markets more stable. Investment history is full of examples of how not keeping a strong focus on being diversified led to disaster. We can go all the way back to the 1970s, for example. Coming into the 1970s, things were great. The 50 largest stocks were considered the "Nifty Fifty," one-decision stocks. Buy them and forget them, because they would only go up. Many investors did exactly that. Then came OPEC, inflation, and the resignation of the U.S. President. The American mood and the markets turned sour. As markets collapsed, losses mounted and people panicked. At the bottom, they sold the stocks they owned. Warren Buffett was one of the few who kept a cool head and bought stocks as prices hit rock bottom. He pounced on the bargains offered by panicky sellers. When the market crashed in October 1987, investors who had all their money in stocks got scared and sold. As a disciplined practitioner of asset allocation and diversification, Yale University was ready to tactically reallocate right after the 1987 selloff, from bonds and cash into stocks at what turned out to be historically low levels. More than five years after the 2000–2002 tech stock bubble burst, the memory of the tech bubble remained vivid for many investors still suffering from embracing the new paradigm too tightly. In chasing hot investments and ignoring diversification in favor of the financial lottery ticket that tech stocks seemed to offer, investors exposed themselves to financial heartbreak and still wary, missed a lot of the 2003–2007 stock price recovery.

If you have your eggs in more than one basket, you will be subject to fewer extreme mood swings, from despondency when everything seems to be moving down in price, to euphoria when everything seems to be moving up in price, that may cause you to do exactly the wrong thing at the wrong time. In the late 1990s, investors who practiced asset allocation and paid attention to keeping their portfolios diversified were selling tech stocks to buy underpriced assets such as real estate investment trusts and bonds that subsequently did very well. The oft-cited mantra of Buy Low and Sell High is achieved through diversification. As assets rise and swell to too large a percentage of the portfolio, asset allocation has us selling them and redeploying the money into more out-of-favor sectors and asset classes. Buying Low and Selling High.

We buy low and sell high—the mantra of successful investing—by portfolio rebalancing. By establishing targeted percentages of your total portfolio that are to be placed in stocks, bonds, cash, real estate, and other investments based on your goals, asset allocation is like a navigation system. Along the way, the prices and returns of each investment in the portfolio will fluctuate in varying degrees. If you targeted an asset allocation of 50 percent in stocks and 50 percent in bonds ($50 in stocks and $50 in bonds, for a total portfolio of $100), and after one year, the stocks doubled while the bonds stayed flat, the portfolio would then be 67 percent in stocks and 33 percent in bonds ($100 in stocks and $50 in bonds, within a total portfolio of $150). To get back to the originally targeted 50–50 mix of equities and bonds, you will reallocate so that $75 is in stocks and $75 is in bonds. To do this, you would sell $25 out of the $100 stocks portfolio and with the proceeds buy $25 of additional bonds. This process is called *rebalancing the portfolio*. Buy Low, Sell High.

You can rebalance in either one of two ways: by price or by time. When an asset allocation is rebalanced to its target mix by time, you will allow the various asset classes in the portfolio to experience their upward or downward price changes until a predetermined amount of time has passed. The rebalancing is then carried out to arrive at the originally targeted asset allocation. The time period could be annual, semiannual, quarterly, or some other interval. The time frame will be based on how involved you wish to be and your attitude toward the markets and the economy. Although the by-time approach may lead to some degree of variation from the originally targeted asset allocation, this method may incur lower transaction costs than a rebalancing rule driven entirely by asset price changes. That is the other way to rebalance your portfolio. You simply rebalance your portfolio back to the original target allocations as soon as they experience a specified percentage deviation from the original percentages. For example, 5 percent, 10 percent, or some other percentage change might trigger a rebalancing to get back to the originally targeted asset allocation. Such a rebalancing rule tends to keep the portfolio fairly closely aligned with its originally targeted allocation, but at the same time, this method may require a closer level of portfolio monitoring and may generally incur greater transaction costs due to the possibility of more frequent asset percentage adjustments than the by-time approach.

The asset allocation approach to investing has one other enormous benefit. As we put together a portfolio and decide which assets we will or will not use to meet our goals, we are forced to think about risk in real terms. We all talk about risk in much the same way that we talk about eating a healthy diet, but few of us really do anything about it. Okay, so you understand that investing involves risk. Ask yourself how much you could stand to lose. No, really. How much can you take? How much of a loss can you withstand according to your goals? Can you take a loss on the money you are saving to buy a vacation home? How much would you be willing to lose, over what time frame, for your children's college fund? What about your retirement? Now, what would be worse—losing that much money, or not gaining a certain amount? Asset allocation can't make risk go away. Face it, life is full of risks and success is not a straight line up. What asset allocation does is force you to ask and answer some challenging questions which should lead you to a portfolio construction that will, hopefully, prevent you from doing something silly when things get tough, or when things are going exceedingly well. (It is often said that, due to euphoria, investors make more mistakes during bull market times than they do in bad times due to euphoria.) If you hold different types of investments, then your asset allocation strategy will bring a degree of realism to the investment process, in which you ask yourself whether the glass is half empty or half full. The arithmetic of risk and loss is well known. An asset that declines 50 percent in price (for example, from $100 down to $50), has to increase by 100 percent in price (from $50 back up to $100) just to get back to even. If you have truly diversified your portfolio so that all the investments' prices are not moving in the same direction at the same time, asset allocation should dampen the overall effects of a price decline in some investments. You do not want to find yourself wishing and hoping and praying that your capital will increase by 100 percent to get back to even; this *rarely* happens.

Being aware of risk does not eliminate risk or help you avoid risk, but it is usually better to think beforehand about how much risk you are willing to take, how you can build in a margin of safety wherever possible in selecting assets, and how you might react to capital losses. Some people go into denial; some get frozen into inaction; and some remain calm, dispassionate, and rational when faced with losses. No matter how you respond to loss, asset allocation can fortify your psyche through prior contemplation of risk and by moderating the overall effects of a specific asset's loss when viewed in the context of the portfolio as a whole. In other words, by planning beforehand for a worst-case scenario, you can take whatever the winds may toss your way and avoid knee-jerk reactions that tend to make matters worse. It's just not wise to try and formulate an escape plan during a fire at the same time everyone is rushing for the exits.

One of the primary advantages of asset allocation is reduced price volatility. That in turn reduces the risk for your portfolio as a whole because some assets may be doing well when other assets are not doing so well, and some portions of your portfolio may not be doing as well as others. But that's okay. You planned for some tough moments in your child's college fund. You can take a downswing in that S&P 500 fund you are invested in because those funds are set aside for college tuition that won't need to be paid for another 15 years. It's like spreading your bets on several teams, rather than putting yourself in an all-or-nothing situation by backing only one team. The best part is it's putting the right bets on the right teams. You don't want to bet on a baseball team going to the Super Bowl. First, they don't play football; second, they may have been trying for almost 100 years to win a baseball championship! It's the same with your investments.

Asset allocation can seem like a complicated concept. All it really is, is selecting a portfolio of investments that will work together to make your realistic goals more attainable. It is not a get-rich-quick method by any stretch of the imagination. It is a method for approaching yourself and the markets rationally, and using available tools to build a portfolio that will shield you from taking on too much risk and volatility. When asked what the most powerful force in the universe was, Albert Einstein replied simply, "Compound interest." Asset allocation gives us the staying power to allow compound returns over time to work their powerful magic to make our investment goals a reality.

Chapter Two

Everyone Needs
an Uncle Frank

~

*We All Need Someone
to Lean On*

THERE ARE UNCLE FRANKS everywhere. Athletes who win the big game are always thanking the high school coach who taught them to hone their skills and who they still call for advice. Memoirs of successful people in every field of endeavor cite an individual they turned to for advice and insight in the matters of business and life. The great investors all have one or two Uncle Franks. Consider

Warren Buffett. His original Uncle Frank was Ben Graham. When Graham retired, he adopted a new Uncle Frank in the person of Charlie Munger. Uncle Frank is the single most valuable resource you will have as you set up your asset allocation plan and begin the journey to try to turn your dreams into reality. You will find yourself turning to him for advice, motivation, and encouragement. Whenever you are considering which asset classes or specific investments to use, you will need an independent objective source, a trusted friend to help guide you. In short, you need an Uncle Frank.

How do you recognize an Uncle Frank (or an Aunt Sally)? Many times, but not always, you find that you naturally seek these people out on important life and investment decisions. You listen to them. You get along with them, even though you may not always like or agree with what they say to you. You do this because you sense that your Uncle Frank has your best interests in mind and wants to see you do well in life. Another reason you are comfortable with your Uncle Frank is that there is not a trace of envy, jealousy, or rivalry in the relationship between you.

Your Uncle Frank (who may very well be your Aunt Sally) is comfortable with himself or herself and possesses some degree of experience, and usually has attained a measure of success in life. They tend to complement you and bring out the best in you. They genuinely like you, encourage you, and often provide mental and emotional support in difficult times and markets.

Uncle Franks are rare and don't grow on trees. Many times, it can take quite a while for you to realize who your Uncle Frank is. Uncle Frank may be a cousin, a grandparent, a niece, a nephew, or a neighbor. Although your Uncle Frank may be a coworker or a spouse, it's frequently the case that close proximity does not guarantee the conditions for an Uncle Frank–type relationship. Your Uncle Frank may or may not be in the investment business.

Whether your Uncle Frank has known you for a long time, he is pretty good at spotting your strengths and weaknesses. Your Uncle Frank has an uncanny ability to augment your strengths and minimize your weaknesses. He can often inspire you to make the best of what resources you have and take your game to the next level.

Uncle Frank knows that the current price of an asset is not necessarily what it's worth. It may be worth far more or far less than it trades for today, and Uncle Frank is very good at helping you see the difference and appropriately take advantage of the resulting opportunity. He is market-savvy and knows when you should press your advantage with a successful investment and when to cut your losses with an unsuccessful one. Your Uncle Frank has a definitive set of investment beliefs, and his knowledge can help you translate thought into investment action.

Your Uncle Frank recognizes that it is human to err and that everyone is going to make investment mistakes. Equally importantly, he always seeks to learn from investment mistakes and tries to avoid repeating them. Without discouraging you, your Uncle Frank is nevertheless not shy about throwing cold water on any of your grandiose, pie-in-the-sky asset allocation and investing schemes that have no chance of turning out the way you have deluded yourself into thinking they will. Your Uncle Frank wants you to achieve your realistic goals by dealing in reality and meaning rather than in words and dreams. He takes time to ask what can go wrong in an asset allocation and/or an investment strategy.

For you to get the best out of your Uncle Frank, you need to be honest and open with him. You need to be respectful of his time, and you need to give him concrete evidence and feedback, showing that you hear and understand his message. In turn, there are a number of qualities and attributes you should seek from your Uncle Frank.

Your Uncle Frank can help you understand human nature in crowds and your own individual human nature. You want to gain from your Uncle Frank a sense of how markets work when they are functioning normally, how markets behave during periods of high or low volatility, and how investors behave during episodes of extreme optimism or pessimism. You want your Uncle Frank to explain and apply important lessons and conclusions from history.

One of the key reasons you rely on an outside person in asset allocation and investment matters is to help you separate the signal from the noise in all the short-term and long-term information that comes your way from the worlds of finance, economics, and politics. Sometimes, a conversation with your Uncle Frank can help you make judgments about what is really happening. You should seek Uncle Frank's views and viewpoints to heighten and focus your curiosity about cause-and-effect relationships and how things work in the world. Another insight your Uncle Frank can help you with is knowing the difference between luck and skill in your investment successes.

As investors, we need to know where markets are today, where they are in the current business cycle, and where they are from a long-term perspective. With his knowledge of where markets are right now and in a historical context, Uncle Frank can help you see when prices and trends might be likely to reverse or continue in their current direction.

Your Uncle Frank remembers the words of John Maynard Keynes, the famous British economist: "Markets can remain irrational for longer than you can remain solvent." Quite often, we may buy a little too soon and sell a bit early. At times, much patience is required while we watch our asset and investment decisions play out. Patience may be one of the most difficult investment virtues to practice. As a trusted outsider, Uncle Frank can help you develop the patience, calm, and reason you need to achieve success with your decisions.

None of us is ever going to be able to allocate assets and select investments with complete and perfect information. In our modern world, the quantity of information that reaches us has exhibited dramatic growth, from blogs and other Internet-based sources to financial radio and TV. We have newspapers, market letters, chart services, columns, reports, and releases from an ever-growing number of sources. We need help funneling all this data and noise down to useful information. We need to separate the proverbial wheat from the chaff. Uncle Frank can help us do this. He can help us determine which information is useful to the asset allocation process and which information should be ignored.

In times of market turbulence and volatility, your trusty Uncle Frank can help you keep a clear head and make correct decisions. He can help you deal with the bouts of panic and euphoria that often occur in financial markets. He is direct. He is honest. He is knowledgeable about life as well as finance and economics. He knows you. Uncle Frank can help you keep your hand on the tiller sailing toward your dreams.

Chapter Three

Building Your House

Your Portfolio, like Your House,
Needs to Reflect Your Personality

IN MANY WAYS, putting together a portfolio is like buying and decorating a house. Families will have different housing demands, and within every house each room will have its own purpose. When we shop for a home, we need to have an idea of how many rooms we would like to have and how we plan to use each room, in addition to how we want the rooms to look. If we don't think about these things in advance, we may well end up with a house that is too big or too small, with furniture and fixtures that are faddish, or something a salesperson pushed on us that doesn't work for us. We might get a couch that looks great in our neighbor's living room but doesn't fit ours at all. We might end up with a refrigerator that works for the newlyweds next door but isn't big enough to accommodate our family of five.

It's the same with putting together a portfolio. My portfolio will differ from yours, which will be different from your best friend's or your brother's—even if we are all similar in age. We need to have some idea of what assets—the furnishings—we are going to use and how we are going to position them. Then we can look at whatever hot new product is being pitched to us by the financial industry. It, like hot pink wallpaper, may be absolutely perfect for us or it could be a huge mistake. Just because your good friends have an investment they are excited about does not mean it will fit in your portfolio. We need to be aware of the special characteristics and uses of each asset class so we don't end up with a portfolio full of the investment equivalent of lava lamps and shag rugs—or even fine but oversized furniture that doesn't fit our rooms. We need to keep in mind that just as a dining room table can run the gamut in quality from pressed wood to the finest cherry, there can be a wide range of quality within each asset class.

Uncle Frank Says . . .

Make sure the assets in your portfolio suit your needs and your personality, just as your furniture fits a room and your own individual style.

People have varying motivations, financial reasons, and emotional needs—ranging from greed to fear, from comfort to unfamiliarity—that affect their investment decisions. Why we buy what we buy is based on a host of different factors. The major types of assets (the kinds of furniture for our house) and the most common reasons for owning them are shown in Exhibit 3.1.

For our home to be all we want it to be, some of the rooms need to be for the good times. This is the television room with our big screen and wet bar. In terms of our portfolio, this room contains assets that do well in prosperous economic and financial times. We will have rooms that are for relaxing and feeling safe. The bedrooms of our portfolio need to contain assets that tend to flourish in difficult economic and financial circumstances (such as a tough business environment, high inflation, deflation, or unsettled political and geopolitical conditions). Some rooms have specific functions in the house. Our portfolio's kitchen needs to have characteristics that are

Exhibit 3.1   Major Asset Classes and Common Reasons for Owning Them

Asset Class	Represents Investors' Quest for
Cash	Safety, Security, Liquidity, Income
Bonds	Income, Reliability, Predictability, Priority, Growth, Satisfaction of Known Liabilities
Stocks	Ownership, Linkage to Value Creation, Economic Gain, and Profits
Real Estate	Tangibility, Ownership, Ego, Gain, Income
Commodities	Exposure to the Satisfaction of Elemental Human Needs, Anticipation of Price Moves
Precious Metals	Purchasing Power Protection, Permanence, Refuge in Unsettled Conditions
Private Equity/Venture Capital	Capital Growth, Influence and Control over Corporate Destiny
Managed Futures	Trend Exploitation, Protection against Financial Market Turbulence
Hedge Funds	Finding and Taking Advantage of Marketplace Inefficiencies
Inflation Indexed Securities	Inflation Hedge, Purchasing Power Protection
Art	Prestige, Rarity, Associativeness, Ego, Intellectual Affirmation

functional during all kinds of times. Think of it this way: If your television goes on the fritz, you can read a book, play chess, or go ride a bike. If your oven fails, you will either eat cold food or be forced to go out for dinner (or call for delivery), thus incurring greater costs just to feed you and your family.

Uncle Frank Says . . .

Match the investment to the goal.

For your home to be functional and comfortable and look the way you want it to, the rooms have to meet their specific functions in a manner that appeals to your sensibilities—not your neighbor's or your mother's. You are the one who has to live with your house and your portfolio. For your portfolio to thrive over the long term, you need to generally have a mix of functional, relaxing, and enjoyable investments. From time to time, things will change and you might turn a spare bedroom into an office. Similarly, you may well vary your investment selections based on changing conditions. Solid asset allocation should serve your needs, protect you from the elements, appreciate in value over the years, and not cost you too much financially or in headaches to maintain. (The motto of your asset allocation should be the same as that of the

U.S. Postal Service and deliver in snow, rain, heat, or gloom of night.)

At its most basic level, asset allocation involves gaining an understanding of which asset classes work best together and which separately; for whom; under what circumstances; for how long; and at what explicit and implicit costs and risks. Again, it's a lot like furnishing a house. What fabrics look good together and which ones clash? Do I have to go to an upscale store to get what the room needs or will Ikea work for me? Does that knick-knack I found at the flea market actually fit in the room or will it look ridiculous?

Understanding what each type of asset can and cannot do for us involves answering some basic questions. In investment terms, how has this asset class performed (and how might it be expected to perform) in good times, in bad times, or in so-so times? Does this type of investment respond primarily to interest rate movements, to underlying supply-demand conditions, or to what another investor is willing to pay for it? Will the asset's return come in the form of income, capital gains, or both? How big or small might the gains realistically turn out to be? How wide are the daily, weekly, monthly, yearly, and multiyear fluctuations in returns? Do the swings matter to me? Does this asset class tend to perform similarly or differently from other asset classes? Over what usual time frame are returns generated? How predictable or unpredictable are the returns? How easy will it be to find out about, understand, access, enter, own, keep track of, pay taxes on, and sell this investment?

Are all parts of the asset class pretty much alike? For example, Treasury bonds as an asset class contain only various maturities of—you guessed it—U.S. Treasury bonds. Other asset classes such as stocks and real estate may vary widely in quality and characteristics. Does the asset class contain many subcategories and variations? Is this kind of asset class primarily available in my domestic market or in a foreign setting? How is the asset created? What types of investors like to invest in this asset class? What kinds of forces cause them to buy and sell?

Recognizing that history does not always unfold in repeatable patterns (no one rings a bell when market and economic cycles change), a fixed approach probably won't serve most people through all market cycles. Yet it is still helpful to keep in mind how each type of investment has tended to perform under a range of market conditions. These areas of relative asset class *emphasis* (and thus, relative *de-emphasis* of other asset classes) are nicely shown in an asset allocation clock I've developed that I call the *asset allocation clock* (Exhibit 3.2).

The asset allocation clock shows that, in general, it is a good idea to focus on equity-like assets during periods

Exhibit 3.2   Asset Allocation Clock

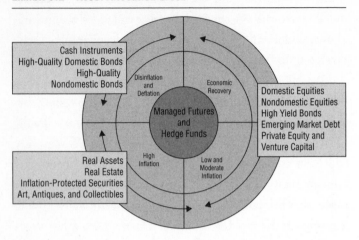

of economic growth and low to moderate inflation. By doing this, you will emphasize real, nonfinancial assets (such as real estate, commodities, and precious metals) during times of high inflation and concentrate on cash investments and high-quality fixed income securities, such as bonds, during episodes of disinflation and deflation. Because of their relatively high degree of opportunism and manager specificity, managed futures and hedge funds (whether accessed individually or through a fund of funds) are placed in the center of the asset allocation clock to signify their potential use (subject to whether these investments are suitable for you) under a fairly broad range of economic and financial conditions.

Let's take a look at the choices we have to furnish our home. Just as each piece of furniture and the decor we choose fits a specific purpose, each asset class has a specific purpose and unique characteristics.

Stocks represent the recreation rooms of the house. This is where we enjoy the good life. An investment in stocks gives us a chance to participate in the good economic times and enjoy the fruits of human endeavor. Just as we all have different ideas of fun and might have different types of furnishings in our recreation or family rooms, stocks have a wide variety of classifications. One person might have a 60- inch flat screen TV and a pool table, whereas another prefers chess boards and another prefers walls of bookcases. TV room, game room, library—each has a different tone and feel, but they are all about enjoying life and leisure. It's the same with stocks. They can be classified by size, by valuation specifics, or by geography, but they have the same general purpose—to capture the best returns while recognizing that price volatility is always a risk.

Bonds and other fixed income investments represent the bedrooms of our house. Here we want to be safe and sheltered from the difficulties of the day. By and large, bonds offer safety and comfort. Keep in mind, however, that just as a Victorian room with a canopy bed is much different from a bedroom with flamboyant red wallpaper and a circular bed, bonds can vary widely in their quality and maturity, ranging from ultra-secure Treasury bonds to high yield, or junk bonds. They all respond to interest rates, but the riskier and longer maturity bonds respond with wider price swings than safer, shorter-term bonds.

Almost every home has a room that is completely different from anyone else's and that reflects some specific taste of its inhabitant. It might be dad's study with an old-fashioned desk, a humidor, and brandy decanter that is totally out of step with the modern tone of the rest of the house. It could be a sitting room off a bedroom with Victorian tones, unlike any other room in the house, that grandma really enjoys when she visits. Alternative investments in the investment world are completely different, just like these rooms. These assets include real estate, private equity, precious metals, or even inflation-protected securities. They may seem odd in an otherwise conventional portfolio of stocks and bonds, but they fill a specific need. Returns here might be a result of inflation or manager skill. What these types of investments all have in common is that their returns are usually generated by forces that are different from the forces affecting our more traditional stock and bond investments, making them a good choice for diversification.

Some of the rooms in your house are more mundane but no less important. The basement may not be terrifically exciting or a place where you spend a lot of time, but the hot water heater and electric supply panel are crucial to the smooth operation of the rest of the house. The attic (another infrequently used space) is nonetheless important for its insulation that keeps the home warm in the winter and cool in the summer while reducing stress on the heating and cooling systems. The front closet houses the alarm system wiring that protects your family and belongings from theft. Think of these rooms as the cash component of your portfolio. Cash and cash equivalents are money that is readily available at all times, particularly during the tough spots. It is where we keep the money we know we will need at some point in time to meet a specific need or to have on hand for emergencies.

The way we decorate our house is personal. The art and furnishings we select have value to us for specific reasons. We might think a Monet painting is beautiful and Jackson Pollock a crazed splatter master. What we are willing to pay for something to put on our walls and mantels is driven entirely by how we feel about it. A child's painting can be worthless to a stranger, but quite precious to the child's parents. The arts and collectibles marketplace functions in much the same way. Values are driven by popularity, taste, and by a host of other non-quantifiables. Assets in this market are worth what someone is willing to pay for them—nothing more and nothing less. Some people have an eye for spotting art and antique values, and some are just lucky.

How you purchase, hold, and eventually sell an asset can be as important as *what* you own. The way you invest in specific asset classes tends primarily to be a function of (1) how much money you have relative to the asset's investment minimum purchase amounts, (2) how much time and attention you can devote to investing, (3) your investment experience, and (4) your preferred sources of investment information and advice.

Some people want to decorate their houses on their own. Even if they can afford to pay a professional decorator, they enjoy looking through magazines, going to stores, and examining the options themselves. These types of investors want to select their own stocks and bonds. They like to build their portfolios based on their own research and analysis about specific companies, fund managers, and economic conditions. The advantages of this method are that you get to pick everything: where to shop, how much to spend, and when. It is important to understand that your success depends on your capabilities and knowledge of everything from window coverings to flooring. Likewise, your success in achieving solid investment results is going to depend on your knowledge of markets and individual stocks and bonds. If you are the type who prefers the latest and greatest gadgetry and furnishings, you might well find yourself over budget with a lot of fixtures and bells and whistles you don't need or won't use. You may also find yourself with a sofa that doesn't fit through your door. Doing it yourself means that the entire burden of putting together a high-quality portfolio falls on your shoulders, and you will have to monitor your portfolio closely. If you create a beautiful home but then fail to maintain it, you may find yourself with an albatross you can't unload at any price.

Some people prefer to do most of the decorating themselves with some limited guidance using the low-cost design resources of stores like Home Depot or Ikea. You can set your budget and let someone else do the actual measurements for your kitchen cabinets and windows. You can tell them what you want and let them take it from there. If you are this type of investor, you will likely use mutual funds. By pooling your money with other investors, you gain access to professional, specialized investment management. You pick the kitchen cabinets (value fund or growth fund) and let them take care of the details (which stocks). You pick the type of fund, be it conservative, aggressive, or somewhere in between, and professional managers make the buying and selling decisions to help you reach your goals. When you use store design services, costs will vary. Some stores charge more than others (or their products could cost more than others). Mutual fund fees can be high and detract from long-term returns and need to be considered carefully before investing. Some stores and manufacturers have better schedules than others. Some mutual fund managers do not keep up with the market or the index they are compared against. Performance and fees must be reviewed carefully if you choose to put your portfolio together this way.

Some people just do not want to deal with any part of furnishing a house, and they have enough money to hire a professional decorator to handle everything. These investors use individual money managers or advisors. The drawback here? You have to be able to afford it. The minimum investment for these managers can be quite high; they did not buy the house they live in or their fancy offices because they work cheap.

For some, the costs and fees associated with furnishing a home represent the primary concern. They will shop for the best prices above and beyond all else. For these investors, there are products such as index funds and exchange-traded funds. They are inexpensive and not very fancy, but they are perfectly fine investments that can be used to meet your goals.

There are some types of investments, especially among the alternative investments asset classes, that are a bit like co-ops. They pool investors together in fairly small groups to achieve a specialized purpose. You might buy into a certain co-op to secure a choice address. You might invest through a partnership to gain specific exposure to an asset class such as real estate, timber, oil and gas, or put money with a specific hedge fund or private equity manager.

There are some people who want to do it all themselves, even taking on highly specialized roles. These people serve as their own general contractor and supervise the construction of their homes. They like the feeling of control they have over all aspects of the task. There are investors who want to own their own rental properties. Some investor types prefer direct ownership of commodities or may trade foreign currencies themselves. Just as it takes a lot of knowledge, commitment, and skill to build your own home, it takes specialized knowledge and a large amount of time and skill to manage specialized investments yourself. How you buy and furnish your home depends on a variety of factors, from the level of your commitment and interest to your skills, abilities, and time constraints. In much the same way, how you put your portfolio together will depend on your investment personality, how much money you have to invest, and your time frame.

In the end, one of the most important determinants of how you invest boils down to whether you are structuring the asset allocation or whether someone else is doing it for you. If the latter, you need to devote considerable effort to finding a trustworthy agent. This person will act

Uncle Frank Says . . .

Know yourself and be realistic about your strengths and limitations in using investment tools. Make sure the right person is using the right tools for the specific investment task at hand.

with integrity, represent your interests, devote considerable effort and resources toward structuring and executing an appropriate and successful asset allocation for you, and be as vigilant as you would be in all respects, from the size of your portfolio to expenses to your changing circumstances over time.

Chapter Four

Parts of the Whole—Combining Dreams into a Plan

~

Your Plan Should Be as Specific and Individual as Your Dreams

MOST OF US INVEST IN CERTAIN ASSETS not because of what they are and their unique characteristics, or even their inherent benefits, but because of what they can do for us. What we often do not do is think about exactly why we should buy one type of investment over another to meet a specific goal. I have noticed over the years that when we tell clients they need small-cap stocks or value stocks, for instance, to round out their portfolio, their eyes glaze over. They do not really care so much about what the moving parts of the portfolio are. What they cared about was achieving a specific result. They want to keep their money safe from inflation or market turbulence. They want to send John and Maria to the finest schools. They wanted to buy their dream vacation house, or travel the world, or have money to pay for care for an elderly relative. At the end of the day, do you care how your computer works? Probably not. You just want to know that it will reliably perform the jobs you want it to do.

Stop a moment and think about your portfolio as if it were your computer—doing a job you need it to perform. Does it really matter to you if you own stocks, bonds, timber, or gold? For some people, yes, and for others, not so much. What you care about is having the money to reach your goals. This is why I recommend that you use a method I call *Objective-Based Asset Allocation*. This approach, described in the following paragraphs, allows you to think about what you want your investments to do, exactly and specifically. Objective-Based Asset Allocation forces you to think about why and when a particular type of investment should be added to your overall portfolio. Does the investment relate to your goals, or does it just sound like it promises outsized returns? All too often, I meet people whose portfolio was assembled by buying whatever was hot at the moment, or what a broker was pushing. These portfolios look like an attic of miscellaneous stuff with no thought given to their overall investing goal. Objective-Based Asset Allocation approaches portfolio construction similarly to shopping for a car. We buy cars (at least most of us do, unless we are Jay Leno) according to our needs. We may pay more or less by virtue of our wealth, but we decide on the type of car based on what we need the car to do. Do I drive in the city or country? Do I live in the Southwest or the Midwest? No matter how cute the car, if you need to pull a trailer through snow-covered roads with a fishing boat on it, that Mazda Miata is not going to get the job done.

Look at your investments the same way. For example, if you are looking to fund a college education 18 years from now, you probably want to include growth assets such as U.S. and non-U.S. stocks, real estate, and perhaps precious metals. The goal is long-term capital gains, so you would not want to use bonds for this objective. Although bonds may have fixed interest payments and a promised repayment in the future, they are unlikely to provide the type of long-term appreciation needed to meet your goal. Too many people make the mistake of buying investments without any regard for what they want the investment to do for them (except make money in a very general sense). To my way of thinking, this is the equivalent of sending a baseball player out to play quarterback in his baseball uniform. He may be a great pitcher, but he is probably not going to get the job done on a football field, and more than likely will get hurt.

Uncle Frank Says . . .

Your personal objectives should shape your portfolio.

One of the greatest benefits of using Objective-Based Asset Allocation is that it helps you organize your choices for your portfolio (which may have subportfolios within it, each directed toward a different objective). Picking investments based on objectives will focus your mind on what each asset class can do for you to meet your goals, and how much protection they will give you. If assets are only helpful in relation to our goals and objectives, then we need to know what it is that each type of asset can and can't do for us. This type of approach will help us keep Peyton Manning playing quarterback and Curt Schilling on the pitcher's mound where each is meant to be and under conditions where they are likely to be successful.

There are typically several major investment objectives that investors have in common. The first is *protection against the ravishing effects of inflation.* Exposure to stocks can be a very good hedge against low and moderate inflation. The flexibility of a company to raise prices and grow profits gives it the capacity to perform well in a moderate-inflation economy. However, when inflation rates soar, stocks tend to get hurt. The rising costs of borrowing and doing business make it difficult for them to grow faster than the inflation rate. In addition, many of the models used on Wall Street to value stocks use interest rates as an important input, and the higher interest rates that accompany inflation will make the models lower the overall valuations and eventually the prices of stocks.

The second reason to own stocks and other equity-based assets is *to gain exposure to profitable companies and overall economic growth.* International stocks give us exposure to specific regions of the world outside our domestic market. As growth can be affected by government policies such as taxes and the regulatory climate, owning nondomestic assets can give us exposure to faster-growing economies. In addition, individual companies can be boosted by research and development factors, as well as new products and services. In the long run, owning equity asset classes gives us the opportunity to profit from economic growth. Although life and history do not follow a straight line up, there is no question that the standard of living for most people around the world has improved over time.

Equities allow you to share in the profits of the rising tides that seem to lift all boats, be they the result of demographics, technological advances, or scientific breakthroughs. Diversification among equity asset classes helps us benefit from long-term growth trends.

Third, economies and societies do not always boom when we need the profits most. Sometimes there are difficulties that take a while to work through. Breaks in the upward trajectory of humankind are seen from time to time in recessions, deflating price environments, armed conflicts, and, occasionally, even depressions. All of these are difficult to predict in advance. *Everyone wants to protect their overall portfolio from bad times.* Here, high-quality fixed income assets are the investment class of choice. As long as the fixed income investments are creditworthy and can pay their bills, high-grade bonds, cash investments, and even inflation-indexed securities with their predictable income payments and guaranteed principal should help us weather dangerous economic environments.

Fourth, *at some point we will probably want our portfolio to pay us.* After all, we have worked hard; so too should our money. There are many types of asset classes that can provide income for living expenses, or even for investment in other opportunities. The best assets here include securities such as dividend-paying stocks, preferred stocks, and real estate investment trusts. You might also want to include inflation-indexed securities to generate income flows from the portfolio.

As J.P. Morgan once famously replied when asked about the direction of the stock market: "The one thing we can say for certain is that it will fluctuate." Sometimes wildly. Thus, the fifth common investment objective is *to have a portfolio that doesn't bounce all over the place.* Depending on your risk tolerance and how conservative or aggressive you want to be with your investments, you will want to have some percentage of your portfolio invested in assets that can protect against the volatility and turbulence of equity markets. These might include cash accounts, precious metals, and professionally managed futures funds. There are even some special-purpose hedge funds and exchange-traded funds that can help smooth your returns and protect your portfolio against wild swings. Having investments in your portfolio that help offset the temptation to panic when markets are unsettled can be worth their weight in gold.

Sixth, we now live in a global economy. There is no getting away from this fact, so you need *to have exposure to worldwide currency movements to offset the impact a depreciating currency can have on your investments.* Some investments should be denominated outside your home country. Developed and emerging market stocks and bonds can help us attain this goal. In addition, there are many specialty vehicles, including hedge funds and managed futures funds, that may help achieve this objective.

Now let's talk about the players on our asset allocation team. Each player has unique strengths and weaknesses. I like to think that each asset class has specific characteristics that can help us achieve specific objectives. There are six key investment objectives, and each asset class addresses them differently.

The six major Protection and Exposure objectives for owning a given asset class are shown in Exhibit 4.1, with an "x" indicating whether the 16 asset classes shown in the *rows* meet one or more of the six objectives shown in the *columns*.

The potential advantages and disadvantages that may apply to the 16 most commonly encountered asset classes are shown in the tables in Exhibits 4.2 and 4.3.

We want to be able to mix and match assets that do not act like each other. Real estate, whether real property or real estate investment trusts, behaves differently from assets such as fixed income. Gold tends to differ in behavior from stocks. It is critical to mix and match your assets in order to smooth out your overall portfolio returns.

We want some asset classes that are going to thrive when markets are good. Here stocks, real estate, and other growth assets fit the bill. Certain types of hedge funds also do very well in rising markets.

EXHIBIT 4.1 Protection and Exposure Objectives for Owning an Asset Class

Asset Class	Objective-Based Asset Allocation					
	Inflation Hedge	Economic Growth Exposure	Deflation Hedge	Cash Flow	Volatility Hedge	Currency Risk
Equity						
U.S. Equity	×	×		×		
Europe Equity	×	×		×		×
Developed Asia Equity	×	×		×		×
Emerging Market Equity	×	×		×		×
Fixed Income						
U.S. Fixed Income			×	×	×	
U.S. Short-Term Debt			×	×	×	
High Yield Debt		×				
Developed Non-U.S. Debt			×	×	×	×
Emerging Market Debt			×	×		×
Alternative Investments						
Real Estate and REITs	×	×		×		
Real Assets	×	×			×	×
Private Equity	×	×				
Managed Futures Funds					×	×
Hedge Funds	×	×			×	×
Inflation-Indexed Securities	×		×	×		×
Cash/Cash Equivalents			×	×	×	×

(Continued)

EXHIBIT 4.2 Potential Advantages of Asset Classes

Asset Class	Advantages					
	Low Correlation	Stable Returns	Returns Do Not Track U.S. Equity	Alpha Generated by Manager Selection	Beneficial Liquidity	Inflation Hedge
Equity						
U.S. Equity					X	X
Europe Equity					X	X
Developed Asia Equity					X	X
Emerging Market Equity				X		X
Fixed Income						
U.S. Fixed Income	X	X	X		X	
U.S. Short-Term Debt	X	X	X		X	
High Yield Debt						
Developed Non-U.S. Debt	X	X	X		X	
Emerging Market Debt						

Alternative Investments

	Low Correlation	Stable Returns	Returns Do Not Track U.S. Equity	Alpha Generated by Manager Selection	Beneficial Liquidity	Inflation Hedge
Real Estate and REITs	X			X	X	X
Real Assets	X				X	X
Private Equity/Venture Capital	X		X	X		
Managed Futures Funds	X	X	X	X		
Hedge Funds or Funds of Funds		X	X	X		
Inflation-Indexed Securities	X	X	X		X	X
Cash/Cash Equivalents	X	X	X		X	

Low Correlation: Reflects a weak degree of strength and direction in the relationship of returns between given pairs of asset classes.

Stable Returns: Includes asset classes that exhibit a low statistical dispersion of returns around their average values.

Returns Do Not Track U.S. Equity: Reflects a low degree of sensitivity to U.S. equity returns.

Alpha Generated by Manager Selection: Reflects an investor's ability to augment returns through finding asset managers who can generate returns for a given asset class on a consistent basis above a chosen benchmark.

Beneficial Liquidity: Refers to the ability of an investor to easily enter or exit an investment or to buy and sell an asset in a reasonable period of time without causing a significant upward or downward price movement.

Inflation Hedge: Includes asset classes that tend to guard against high rates of increase in the general price of goods and services (significant fall in the purchasing power of money) within an economy.

EXHIBIT 4.3 Potential Disadvantages of Asset Classes

Assets	Volatility Exposure	High Fees	High Volatility	Liquidity Risk	Disparate Manager returns	Taxation issues	Beta increases with Volatility
Equity							
U.S. Equity	X						X
Europe Equity	X		X				X
Developed Asia Equity	X		X				X
Emerging Market Equity	X		X	X	X		X
Fixed Income							
U.S. Fixed Income							
U.S. Short-Term Debt							
High Yield Debt							
Developed Non-U.S. Debt	X		X	X			
Emerging Market Debt	X		X	X	X		X
Alternative Investments							
Real Estate and REITs	X	X	X	X	X	X	X
Real Assets		X		X	X		

Private Equity/Venture Capital	X		X	X		X	X
Managed Futures Funds		X		X		X	
Hedge Funds or Funds of Funds	X	X		X		X	X
Inflation-Indexed Securities					X		

Cash/Cash Equivalents

Volatility Exposure: Refers to the tendency of an asset to experience significantly unfavorable movements in price, volatility, or liquidity during generally unstable and/or turbulent market conditions.

High Fees: Reflects high costs for asset management, custody, settlement, or for entry into or exit out of a given asset.

High Volatility: Includes assets that exhibit a wide statistical dispersion of returns around their average values. In addition to standard deviation as a measure of risk, some investors may focus on other downside risk measures including shortfall risk (the risk of exceeding a maximum acceptable monetary loss), semi-variance risk, or target semi-variance risk.

Liquidity Risk: Refers to the difficulty for an investor (1) to enter or exit a specific investment; or (2) to buy or sell an asset within a reasonable period of time without causing a significant price movement. Additionally, there may be an inability to obtain a sufficient degree of initial and/or ongoing information about an investment manager's strategies and/or the positions underlying a specific investment fund or vehicle within a given asset.

Disparate Manager Returns: Refers to a significant spread of returns between the top 25% ranking and the bottom 25% ranking asset managers in an asset class or over a given investment horizon.

Taxation Issues: Refers to the potential for an investor to incur substantial income, capital gains, withholding, excise, estate, unrelated business income (UBI), or other taxes at the federal, state, local, or international level.

Beta Increases with Volatility: Refers to asset classes whose investment performance tends to become highly correlated with the investment performance of other asset classes during times of financial market turbulence, even though under normal market conditions the asset classes may exhibit relatively low correlations of returns with other asset classes.

We will want some part of our assets to be liquid and readily available. Many listed stocks have this advantage, as do most money market and short-term fixed income investments. You will want some of your investments to not only be liquid but also be relatively insulated from price fluctuations.

With some assets, the selection of the right manager can help you achieve substantial extra performance for your portfolio. Such assets include hedge funds and private equity funds. A manager with special expertise in an asset class may be able to provide excess returns that allow you to grow your portfolio at a high rate of return. Managers in certain emerging markets who have specialized, in-depth knowledge may achieve this result as well.

Uncle Frank Says. . .

Never use long-term assets for short-term goals.

When assembling our portfolio, we want to think about which of the six protection and exposure character- istics each asset introduces us to. I've seen too many inves- tors who didn't understand the basic concepts of what assets generally do and don't do. They ended up with port- folios that looked like an odd sports team with quarter- backs and pitchers and goalies. What game did they think they were playing? There is no perfect asset class; each has advantages and shortcomings. The point is to understand the players and what game they are meant to play.

Certain assets, such as private equity, hedge funds, and some types of commercial property real estate investments, can be illiquid and expensive. Many assets will cause your portfolio to be exposed to market turbulence. Foreign and domestic stocks, long-maturity bonds, currencies, and commodities can be quite volatile at times. Take one day as an example: the U.S. stock market opened up strong and climbed over 100 points—perhaps on the news of a financial bailout. It then ended the day down as oil rose to $100 a barrel. Yet just a few short years earlier, oil was hardly seen as an investment opportunity, trading below $20 a barrel. U.S. stock returns tend to average about 10 percent a year over the long term, but in the short term the U.S. stock market might be up or down by 20 percent or more in any given year. The stock market is not the only volatile place in the investment world either. Some fixed income assets such as foreign debt and high yield bonds bounce around and can have wildly different returns from year to year.

Some assets that seem very different can begin to act exactly alike in difficult times. Stocks and bonds seem very different at first glance. However, if interest rates rise by a meaningful amount and bonds begin falling in price, stocks may begin to fall as well. Not only is our world global but it is also interconnected.

Some assets such as real estate investment trusts and hedge funds may have a tax disadvantage. In private equity, managed futures, venture capital, and real estate, your returns will depend on the manager.

Now let's take a look at how to make assets work for you in your plan. Let's look at some common objectives and see how the process might work. A common goal for many investors is to fund the ever-growing costs of a college education for their children or grandchildren. Let's assume that Bill and Janie are 4 and 6 years old. We have plenty of time before they are college age, so we'll likely experience several economic cycles before it's time to write tuition checks. Which asset classes do you want to consider? Stocks obviously can help you benefit from the economic growth over the 12- and 14-year time frames you are dealing with. You probably want to consider some foreign stocks to gain some foreign currency exposure and smooth out the overall performance of your stock portfolio. You probably want to consider an allocation to precious metals, inflation-protected securities, and real estate as well to protect against any periods of high inflation. You do not want to be entirely exposed to downside volatility so a portion of your money should go into high-quality fixed income products that will provide some degree of nominal principal protection and steady cash flows to lessen the turbulence.

How about retirement, another common investment goal? If you are a 40-year-old investor, you have a very long time frame. You want many of the same asset classes as in the portfolio set aside to pay for college. Liquidity is not an issue, so you also might want to consider some of the less liquid, high return asset classes such as venture capital, hedge funds, and private equity. Short-term protection against volatility is a little less important, so you might want to decrease the fixed income portion and move that to equities or real estate investment trusts (REITs).

Consider your short-term goals. If you are planning to buy your dream home in five years, you don't have much time and cannot afford to be exposed to price volatility. Here you want to focus on principal-protection cash investments and short-term fixed income instruments. You might want to have a very small allocation to equities to keep up with the economy, but only a very small one. You also want to protect against inflation without the volatility of metals or commodities so inflation-protected securities are worth considering.

A retired investor might approach the process differently. She wants her portfolio to provide the income that makes it possible to enjoy her retirement. If she is reasonably healthy and in the early stages of her retirement, she still has what is probably a fairly long time frame during which she needs to generate income from the portfolio. Protecting her portfolio from loss and earning some reasonable income are more important than the growth of the portfolio. For her, the emphasis will be on fixed income securities and dividend-paying stocks. Rather than owning volatile real assets, she probably wants to consider inflation-protected securities to guard against inflation. Liquidity is an issue, so she wants to avoid the less liquid asset classes such as hedge funds. Real estate investment trusts can provide some inflation protection and they tend to generate dividend income, so these assets should probably be included.

Whatever your dreams, break them down by individual goals. Once you have done this and allocated the proper percentages of assets for each goal, you have something special. You will have created an asset allocation plan that fits you and is designed to accomplish your objectives. By combining all the individual allocations for each goal, you have a road map for your overall portfolio that is goal-specific.

Uncle Frank Says . . .

Think about the timing of your liquidity needs and about how much asset price volatility you can withstand.

Chapter Five

Two Strategies to Win the Battle for Investment Survival

---— ∽ ---—

Use the Current Environment to Keep the Big Picture in Focus

IN THE EARLY 1980s, I was introduced to two brothers who had each inherited a few million dollars from their mother, an electronics whiz. Before she passed away, she sold her company for cash to a big U.S. computer firm. Feeling somewhat traumatized by the volatile, sideways stock market behavior of the 1970s, the older brother put all of his money into a buy-and-hold portfolio of municipal bonds. Throughout the years, he has told me repeatedly that he has managed to live off the bonds' interest income each year, and he and his wife still have the same amount his mother bequeathed to him. In essence, he has used a one-decision strategic asset allocation policy, and he does not react when I remind him that the purchasing power of his money is probably no more than a third of the purchasing power of the money his mother left him.

By contrast, the wife of the younger brother was interested in investments and as time passed, she assumed full responsibility for her husband's portfolio, making it grow through judicious tactical adjustments combined with an overall strategic approach focused on diversification, rebalancing, and reinvestment into U.S. stocks, then non-U.S. stocks, real estate securities, precious metals, commodities, and high-grade bonds. After 2000, she added managed futures, hedge funds, and inflation-protected securities. Recently she showed me the value of her portfolio—it was more than *seven times* the value of the brother-in-law's!

Some of their relative success can be attributed to luck and fortuitous timing, but much of the portfolio's approximately 8.5 percent compounded rate of growth over the 25 years we are talking about came from the basic blocking-and-tackling skills of strategic and tactical asset allocation and their powerful corollaries: diversification, rebalancing, and reinvestment.

There are two basic approaches to asset allocation: You can be strategic about it or you can take a tactical view. Whichever one you use will depend a lot on your objectives and to a greater degree on your personality.

Let's first talk about strategic asset allocation. Great chess masters look at the chess board in terms of a field, and think many moves ahead. In a lot of ways, they play the match out before it ever starts. Playing chess is much like Strategic Asset Allocation, where you set long-term percentage weightings for the assets in your portfolio and maintain the mix for long periods of time. The portfolio is only adjusted (or rebalanced) when the target percentages increase or decrease. There is a bit of Rip Van Winkle or Sleeping Beauty involved here. I tend to think of Strategic Asset Allocation as something of a "set it and forget it" approach to investing.

Tactical Asset Allocation, on the other hand, takes a more responsive view toward your portfolio so that the asset mix is adjusted to try to gain benefit from underlying market and economic trends. In chess terms, a strategic approach wins the match, but the tactical moves get us there based on what our opponent has just done.

Your Strategic Asset Allocation plan represents the long-term, big-picture view that will take you from Toronto to, say, Florence. But why are you going on this trip? Is it for vacation or business? Do you plan to fly, go by ship, or use some combination of transport means (you could fly to Rome and then drive to Florence, for instance)? A Strategic Asset Allocation plan answers where you are going and why and then generally defines what methods you'll use to get to your final destination. Strategic Asset Allocation helps you set the general asset mix based on which investments are most likely to achieve your goals, consistent with your tolerance for risk and your time horizon.

In fundamental terms, Strategic Asset Allocation functions as a sports team's coach: selecting assets for the portfolio as well as deciding when not to use certain assets. This approach attempts to produce the best possible investment performance in various economic and financial market environments. Just as a coach relies on statistical as well as qualitative considerations when putting together a team for an entire playing season, a well-founded Strategic Asset Allocation plan draws on important historical and fundamental aspects of you, the investor, and the asset classes at your disposal.

A portfolio's Strategic Asset Allocation consists of the long-term investment weightings for the core asset classes that best respond to your goals, return objectives, and risk profile and that take into account an asset's returns, its volatility, and how it behaves compared to other asset classes under various economic and financial conditions. You want the mix that is best suited to your dreams *and* your personality.

Uncle Frank Says . . .

The big picture is strategic. Today is tactical.

Strategic Asset Allocation can help you match the structure of your portfolio with your objectives. Such financial goals might include generating income to pay bills and maintain your lifestyle in retirement, growing capital to meet long-term objectives such as a child's education, or keeping your principal safe from turbulent times in the financial markets during retirement.

Using a Strategic Asset Allocation plan helps us stay focused on our long-term goals. It helps us develop a reasoned, thoughtful approach to meet our long-term financial objectives. This type of plan helps us ask questions that we might overlook when selecting our investments. Is this investment in my long-term best interest? Will it help me accomplish the purpose of my investment portfolio? What is the purpose of my investment portfolio? What can go wrong? Before setting out on a journey, it is a good idea to think carefully about where you want to go, when you want to get there, and the best means of travel. A Strategic Asset Allocation plan can act like a navigational beacon, allowing us to steer our portfolio in the long-term direction originally established.

Uncle Frank Says . . .

Pay attention to the two most often-overlooked influences of your overall portfolio results: taxes and expenses.

An often overlooked benefit of using Strategic Asset Allocation is that it reduces the overall costs of investing. Many asset classes have fairly high costs associated with buying and, in particular, selling, as well as substantial tax implications. By considering the impact of these costs up front when designing your strategic asset mix, you can avoid costly mistakes later on. In addition, some assets such as hedge funds, private equity, venture capital, and real estate cannot always be disposed of quickly. If you are going to need access to your money, or are simply uncomfortable with illiquid investments, consider these factors before you buy them. (Don't forget that an investment's return is only "earned" when you sell the asset; the rest of the time, the gains exist only on paper.) You may well decide to limit your exposure to illiquid investments. As you pursue your goals, Strategic Asset Allocation is meant to raise your awareness of the costs of excessively switching from asset to asset or buying assets that are difficult to sell.

Another of the most important advantages of Strategic Asset Allocation is that it helps us avoid the twin scourges of successful investing: fear and greed. By having a firm plan and preset allocations to the types of investments you own, you are better able to avoid the temptation to buy in rising markets and sell when prices are falling. In fact, following your allocations tends to force you to do the opposite and buy low, sell high—which is the point of investing! Buy Low, Sell High. What great advice! There will always be bull markets, financial fads, and hot tips at cocktail parties. The road to ruin is littered with the remains of bad investments made for the wrong reasons. Following a Strategic Asset Allocation plan keeps us on a more heavenly path.

Uncle Frank Says . . .

Keep your eye on the Big Picture, but watch your step!

Merely having a Strategic Asset Allocation plan is not a guarantee of success, of course. For example, when the Penn Central Railroad bankruptcy of June 1970 and the first OPEC oil price increase of October 1973 (from $1.00 per barrel to $4 per barrel!) occurred, many investors thought these were indications that the U.S. economy was on a recessionary path that would lead to *lower* interest rates. Such people might have structured their Strategic Asset Allocation so that long-term bonds dominated their portfolios. Sounded reasonable at the time, I'm sure. Except that these investors would have suffered significant losses as interest rates on 10-year U.S. Treasury bonds instead *rose* to over 15 percent in 1981! In this case, the Strategic Asset Allocation was based on incorrect assumptions, which led to the wrong course of action for a decade or more. Such traumatic investment experiences may also produce investment paralysis or capitulation at just the wrong time, when decisiveness and radical rethinking would have been far more appropriate.

Strategic Asset Allocation thinking can also be so long term in nature and outlook that highly attractive investment prospects may be overlooked. For example, high yield (junk) bonds sometimes tend to undergo prolonged periods of outperformance, followed by equally prolonged periods of underperformance. This type of long-term volatility makes them unsuitable for many buy and hold investors. A rigid adherence to long-term views may cause you to miss tremendous opportunities when the high yield market generates several years of spectacular returns. This type of long-term volatility, with periods of high profit opportunities, can be seen in many commodity markets. These types of investments would be off limits to the long-term buy and hold investor, but might otherwise make perfectly good sense to help meet portfolio objectives.

Another problem with Strategic Asset Allocation planning is that it may be perfectly appropriate for one kind of investor, at a certain age and of a certain net worth, who has a specific outlook on the economy and the long-term potential of the financial markets, but can quickly become inappropriate when conditions change. If you are not paying attention, you and your life may change, but you forget to change your Strategic Asset Allocation plan. People get older, and their health changes. They get married; they get divorced. The kids grow up, graduate from college, and have their own children. Career circumstances change. An election or geopolitical event can change their outlook on the world to the point that they want to become more conservative or more aggressive in their asset allocation. They may get restricted stock and options from their employer that drastically change their financial circumstances. They could inherit money. It takes time to formulate a Strategic Asset Allocation plan that reflects your goals, situation, point of view, and investment outlook, but it is not set in stone for eternity. As the eminent British economist John Maynard Keynes is reported to have said, "When the facts change, I change my mind. What do you do, sir?" Good judgment, an open mind, and flexibility are essential components of successful Strategic Asset Allocation.

Tactical Asset Allocation can be a helpful response to the potential shortcomings of Strategic Asset Allocation. You need a big plan, but it needs to be reviewed and adjusted from time to time. Tactical Asset Allocation represents the specific maneuvers that force you to keep your eye on the big picture while being agile in response to changing conditions—yours and the rest of the world's. When you go on a trip, you have an itinerary. You know where you want to go. You have a general plan. All too often—and increasingly if you travel by air—trips do not go exactly according to plan. Flights are delayed, roads are closed, baggage is lost, so we have to adjust our plans. You make tactical shifts to your asset allocation weightings in anticipation of changing conditions, be they personal circumstances or significant market or economic forces. Tactical Asset Allocation is also used to take advantage of major shifts in asset valuations. When it is deemed appropriate to do so, you execute Tactical Asset

Allocation shifts by moving asset class weights above (overweight) or below (underweight) your Strategic Asset Allocation weighting to take advantage of what are considered to be short-term movements in asset prices.

Uncle Frank Says . . .

Change happens. Count on it.

Tactical Asset Allocation tends to focus your attention on finding and emphasizing asset classes with significant profit opportunities, and identifying and deemphasizing asset classes that are expected to generate minimal or negative profits. Rather than adopt a "set it and forget it" asset allocation approach, Tactical Asset Allocation seeks to establish whether the price of an asset is above or below its justifiable value. Knowing your own strengths and weaknesses is important in making tactical moves. A large part of your success in using Tactical Asset Allocation is the ability to determine what an asset's true, intrinsic value is at a given point in time; how far out of line the asset's price is versus its true, intrinsic value; and what conditions will make it return to its value. Another benefit of Tactical Asset Allocation is that it causes you to review your portfolio weightings more frequently. This can occur even within specific asset groups. For example, if you felt strongly that U.S. interest rates were going to fall soon, you might adjust your Treasury bond portfolios to favor longer-term bonds. Your allocation to that asset class hasn't changed, but the internal mix of it has. Tactical Asset Allocation may be implemented for only a few assets in the portfolio, or it may be carried out as part of a more thorough portfolio rebalancing.

You can rebalance your portfolio by selling off assets that have been performing well in price (which have grown to represent a larger-than-targeted percentage of the overall portfolio) and buying additional amounts of assets that have declined in price (which having shrunk, now represent a smaller-than-targeted percentage of your overall portfolio). Buying Low and Selling High all over again.

Remember that portfolio rebalancing tends to work best over time periods in which assets' price performance tends to go back to average. Investment professionals use the fancy expression *revert to the mean*. This means that assets that *outperform* their long-term average returns for a period of time will at some point begin to *underperform* their long-term average returns, and assets which *underperform* their long-term average returns for a period of time will at some point begin to *outperform* their long-term average returns. For example, if your stocks were soaring to outsized highs in 1999, a Tactical Asset Allocation plan would likely have indicated that it was time to sell some of those stocks and buy more bonds, whose returns had drifted down well below their historical average. As it turns out, that would have been the right thing to do.

Economic and financial market conditions undergo change during time periods of varying length, from expansion and bullish rising asset prices to contraction and bearish falling asset prices. Tactical Asset Allocation seeks to position your portfolio to take advantage of anticipated economic and financial market developments, whereas your Strategic Asset Allocation seeks to point you in the right direction. Tactical Asset Allocation is like making regular adjustments to your driving style, slowing down for turns in the road and speeding up on the straightaway. Strategic Asset Allocation is what puts you on the highway in the first place, pointed toward Los Angeles or Vancouver or wherever you are headed.

Uncle Frank Says . . .

Tactical does not mean excessive!

If you get too emotionally caught up in the process of making short-term asset allocation adjustments to your portfolio, you may find yourself buying assets when prices are high and selling assets when prices are low. This is precisely the opposite of what should be done. Watching your portfolio too closely and attaching too much importance to the process of Tactical Asset Allocation can be like looking in the oven every couple of minutes to see if the soufflé has risen. Such frenetic behavior leads to intensified feelings of euphoria and mastery when the assets in the portfolio are doing well, and deepens the sense of gloom, despair, and loss when the assets in the portfolio are experiencing difficulty. Opening the oven door constantly on a soufflé will cause it to fall in on itself. Mood swings do not lead to calm, reasoned analytical decision making, but usually produce error-prone shoot-from-the-hip investing activity.

When done right, Tactical Asset Allocation helps capture rewarding investment opportunities without generating an excessive degree of portfolio turnover. When done improperly, Tactical Asset Allocation leads to fidgety, hyperactive buying and selling, generating high transaction costs, and in many cases, high tax bills that eat into the net investment returns produced by the portfolio. High turnover rates also tend to shorten the amount of time you have to weigh the pros and cons of a specific asset relative to its own and other assets' potential in light of market conditions.

A significant potential drawback of Tactical Asset Allocation relates to getting so caught up in short-term trends that you lose sight of the important long-term forces that define and determine success or failure in attaining your asset allocation objectives. When you make this mistake, you miss the forest for the trees. For example, investors who congratulated themselves on capturing the high current yields offered by short-term cash instruments such as Certificates of Deposit (CDs) in the early 1980s may have missed out on participating in two of the greatest bull markets of the twentieth century: the U.S. bond bull market from 1981–2003 and the U.S. equity bull market from 1982–2000. Tactical Asset Allocation should not be another name for hyperactive, expense-generating, short-term trading activity; rather, it should represent reasoned, opportunistic portfolio shifts to capitalize on temporary divergences between assets' prices and their underlying values.

In short, aim high to see the big picture (Strategic Asset Allocation), while at the same time keeping your eyes open to each step you take (Tactical Asset Allocation).

Chapter Six

Do You Know Where You Are Going?

Your Roadmap to Success. Don't Leave Home without It

THE SINGLE MOST IMPORTANT FACTOR in determining how you manage your investments and structure your asset allocation plan is *you*. What do you want out of life? What do you hope to accomplish with your investments? The most important question you can ask yourself is "What is it that I want this portfolio to accomplish?" What is your attitude toward gains and losses? Are you more afraid of losing money, or of missing an opportunity? To successfully establish a portfolio, you have to take some time to get to know yourself and your goals. As the actor Dennis Hopper asks in a popular television commercial, "What are your dreams?" From the start, you need to establish your goals, honestly evaluate your current financial condition, and be aware of your state of mind and feelings about the financial markets. *See pages 193–198 for questions to ask yourself.*

When you think of your investments, what do you see in your mind's eye? Are you watching your son or daughter walk across a stage to take his or her diploma as "Pomp and Circumstance" plays? Are you moving into that big new house on the seventh fairway of the country club? Are you sipping tropical drinks and enjoying a worry-free retirement? Some people see themselves leaving a bunch of money to their favorite charity. Each of us has our own idea of what we want our money to do and exactly why we invest. What do you see? The answer to this question will help shape your investment plans and determine the right way to allocate your assets to make your dreams come true.

When we set our investment goal, we have to consider a number of things. One of the most important is the time frame. How long we have to achieve our goals plays an enormous role in our asset selection. If we are going to need money in two or three years, we must automatically rule out certain asset classes. If Johnny is still toddling around in diapers, we probably don't want to have his college savings in a money market fund. In essence, during the short term, you pay attention to the road you're on and the next few turns you need to make. For the longer term, you pay attention to where you are on the map relative to your final destination.

For teenagers, five to ten years seems like an eternity, but to their parents and grandparents and an investment portfolio, 5, 10, and even 20 years may appear to pass as quickly as a weekend. If we have very long-term goals, then the immediate economic outlook probably won't have much of a bearing on our overall allocation, although it may affect our tactical maneuvers. However, as we age and/or if our goals are closer than, say, a decade away, we need to pay careful attention to the outside forces.

In the long term, our asset allocation plans need to consider the economic outlook and the tone of the decade at hand. The 1980s were different from the 1970s, and the 1990s were completely different from the 1980s. Understanding the economic situation and the state of the markets has an impact on how we develop our plan. What is the current state of the world? Is the planet relatively peaceful? Are there breakthrough technologies and medicines being developed that will radically change the world we live in? What is the trend in taxes? Are the financial markets wildly popular as they were in the 1990s, or are they vilified as they were in the 1970s? The way you structure your portfolio and establish your Tactical Asset Allocation will be influenced by these critical environmental factors. Whatever you want your money to do, you need to have some idea of the economic and sociological background as you put your money to work.

Uncle Frank Says . . .

Your goals are your Constitution; your objectives are your Bill of Rights.

If you're high-minded and directional, asset allocation and investment goals can be compared to a country's Constitution; your asset allocation and investment objectives may be likened to the specifics of its Bill of Rights. Your *goal* is to retire to South Florida. Your *objective* then is to earn 10 percent a year from your investments to make that goal possible. The two most important objectives of any asset allocation and investment activity relate to a portfolio's return and risk.

When we talk about returns in the context of a long-term plan, there are actually two types of returns to consider. The first is the *required return*. This is simply the amount you need on an after-tax basis to keep even with inflation and taxes and pay for your basic needs. The second is the *desired return*. This takes into account inflation, taxes, necessities, and optional outlays for luxuries. In order to distinguish between and calculate the portfolio's required return and its desired return, *you need to determine the annual after-tax inflation-adjusted amount of money you need* to spend on such essentials as food, shelter, education, health care, and other normal living expenses (your required return). A totally separate annual after-tax, inflation-adjusted calculation can be made that includes the required return plus expenditures for optional outlays of a luxury or nonessential nature (your desired return).

Let's walk through the calculations. Exhibit 6.1 shows a representative calculation of the required annual after-tax return needed by an investor who is retired and looks to his or her investment portfolio for income generation. For the purposes of this example, we assume that the investor needs $60,000 in after-tax income per year, and she has a portfolio accounting to $3 million. Step 1 in Exhibit 6.1 shows that her beginning-year after-tax return objective in percentage terms is $60,000 ÷ $3,000,000 = 2%.

Our investor needs a 2 percent return after taxes from her portfolio of $3,000,000 to cover her annual expenses this year of $60,000. What percentage annual return does her portfolio have to generate each year, before taxes, if our investor's overall tax rate at the federal, state, and local

EXHIBIT 6.1   Calculation of Required Annual Portfolio Return

Step 1

$$\text{Beginning-year after-tax return objective in percentage terms} = \frac{\text{Annual after-tax income needs}}{\text{Total portfolio value}}$$

$$\frac{\$60,000}{\$3,000,000} = 2\%$$

Step 2

$$\text{Required ongoing pretax return that takes account of inflation} = \frac{\text{Required after-tax return} + \text{inflation rate}}{(1 - \text{tax rate})}$$

$$\frac{2\% + 2\%}{(1 - 0.30)} = \frac{4\%}{0.70} = 5.72\%$$

level is 30 percent? Step 2 of Exhibit 6.1 also shows how to calculate the required ongoing (annual) pretax return that considers the effects of inflation on our investor's living expenses. To simplify the calculation without introducing a large degree of error, you add the required annual after-tax return to the annual inflation rate in essential or required expenses and divide this percentage by 1 minus the investor's overall tax rate.

We now see that our investor's portfolio needs to generate a pretax annual return of 5.72 percent in order to pay taxes and keep up with the estimated 2 percent inflation rate in her annual living expenses. Generally speaking, given an annual monetary objective that needs to keep up with inflation: (1) the larger the size of the portfolio, the smaller the required return from the portfolio's asset allocation (and conversely, the smaller the size of the portfolio, the larger the required return from the portfolio's asset allocation); (2) the higher the inflation rate in the investor's annual living expenses, the higher the required annual return from the portfolio's asset allocation; and (3) the higher the investor's overall tax rate, the higher the required pretax annual return from the portfolio's asset allocation. Another way to lower the portfolio's annual required return is to lower the absolute monetary amount of the investor's annual expenses. In other words, spend less. Such an adjustment may be relatively easy for some people to accomplish and difficult for others.

Properly understanding and dealing with risk should be as important as thinking about investment returns, but we often downplay or ignore the risks of investing. When we think about risk, we need to be realistic: what can go wrong—or right. There were many big changes in the period from 1989 to 2000. The world was still recovering from the stock market crash of 1987, one of the biggest ever. The early 1990s seemed to usher in a boring quietude to the U.S. markets. But in November 1989, the Berlin Wall had came tumbling down and soon capitalism rose in its place. Following the breakup of the Soviet Union in August 1991, markets rose as the 1990s wore on. But then we saw a new set of disruptive, unexpected forces.

The tech bubble burst, and it seemed as though everything came crashing down. Do not dismiss the events of this period, because similar situations are likely to happen again. The decade from 1997 to 2007 brought us a different world, with both shattering and awe-inspiring events that led to some horrific and great moments. The fact is that something good or bad will almost always happen. It is critical that we be prepared to capitalize on opportunity and deal with adversity. The world changes, and we need to be aware of trends that can affect us, ranging from rising or falling tax rates, to the death of a major political leader such as Mao Tse Tsung, which led to the rise of a free market economy in China. Trends matter, be they good or bad.

Risk tolerance is composed of both your *ability* and your *willingness* to tolerate risk. These two factors may or may not be in sync with each other. Your *ability* to tolerate risk is influenced by the size and form of your net worth, your annual spending needs, and your short-term liquidity needs. Your *willingness* to tolerate risk is influenced by how you acquired your wealth, by past investment and life experiences involving loss and gain, and by your own perceptions of the size of your investment portfolio.

When you have an idea of what you are trying to accomplish, exactly what your dreams are, and what you have to do to make them come true, you need to consider several other factors that are unique to you as you plan your portfolio.

The first of these is your time frame. In general, the longer your time horizon, the greater the degree of portfolio risk you can generally take on. It is important to recognize two things about your time horizon. First, you probably are going to have multiple time frames. You need a new car next year, Jane starts college in 7 years, and your own retirement is 21 years, 7 months, 3 days, and 6 hours away. You also need to be aware that your chronological age is not the same as your income earning age. One 40-year-old might hope to retire at 55 whereas his twin brother plans to work until he is 75. They are the same age but do not have the same investment time frame.

How much you have to invest relative to your spending needs can significantly affect how you allocate your assets. I've encountered people whose way of living and spending requires next to nothing. I've also met well-off individuals who claim they can barely make ends meet as they spend several million dollars a year on multiple estates, jet planes, boats, horse breeding, and other pursuits. Also, how you got your money is important. Did you build a successful business, or was it inherited? Did you work for decades, saving carefully, or did you just have a great run of luck in Las Vegas? Generally speaking, the larger your asset pool, and the greater the degree to which you feel directly responsible for creating your assets, the more risk you might feel comfortable assuming and the greater the share of less liquid, longer-horizon assets you may be willing to include in your asset allocation framework. It's a funny thing (perhaps because they feel they can do it again if necessary) but successful entrepreneurs who sweated the acquisition of each dollar tend to take more risk and a longer-term view. Heirs and heiresses tend to be more conservative in their approach. In many instances, the more aggressive approach (without throwing caution to the wind, of course) prevails over the long term. In a way, Warren Buffett is a high-risk investor in that he buys concentrated positions at low valuations and is prepared to sit on his investments for a long time. But Buffett presumably has the cash on hand to ride out any rough patches.

Several other questions will have a major influence on your required income flows. What is the likely inflation rate for the kinds of expenses you incur? Is your asset base large enough to generate the flows required to cover these expenses? Are you comfortable spending some of your portfolio's principal if necessary to meet your spending needs? What is your overall tax rate, and how might this change over time?

It is important to consider how much liquidity we need in our investments. Some liquidity needs are known. Johnny needs braces for his teeth next year. You will need a down payment for a new house in 18 months. These things you know today. But keep in mind that you may also face unknown liquidity needs (if stuff happens in history all the time, it's logical to assume that stuff will also potentially happen to you). A tree falls on the garage and it needs repair. Jane needs braces for her teeth right now. That cottage at the beach suddenly came up for sale. Dad gets sick. Some portion of your portfolio needs to be in less volatile, readily available investments.

Uncle Frank Says . . .

Do you really have what you need for a rainy day?

Taxes play a large role in our investment plan, too. Your individual tax status is important, and you need to be aware that it can change based on how you earn income and where you live. Each asset class has its own unique tax treatment. You need to consider taxes when determining your asset allocation, but you should also take care not to let tax considerations perversely affect your investment activity. Many times, I have seen investors who know they should sell a highly appreciated asset, but postpone taking action until the gain can be treated as long term by the tax code. Imagine being an investor in July 2007 who had racked up some nice real estate gains but who decided to wait six months to sell with more favorable tax treatment. By December 2007, much of those gains were gone and the asset was difficult to sell, if the property could be sold at all.

Our outlook and general attitude toward investing need to be given some thought. Some people are born bullish and remain that way throughout life. Some people are bearish from their first breath to their last. Another type of person is swayed by external events, the opinions of friends, and the public in general. It doesn't matter what type of person you are. All persuasions can be successful as exemplified by some of the top money managers— some are perennially bearish, some are always bullish, and some change their views, seemingly with the wind. What is important is to ask yourself what type are you, and answer honestly (see pages 193–198). When you see your tendencies clearly, as in golf you can adjust your swing accordingly. If you tend to hit the ball to the right, or always to the left, you can adjust your stance, your swing, or even your aim. If you find that your golf shots scatter in random directions, you can adjust for that, too. Your investment outlook is one of the most difficult things to know and judge about yourself, and wouldn't you know it, it is also one of the most important.

Your investment outlook can be influenced by a number of sources. Friends, brokers, the press, and commentators can influence your thinking. Always be aware of how reliable each is when it comes to financial and economic matters. A statement by Warren Buffett may be a bit more reliable than a tip in an Internet chat room. Is this opinion based on your own research, is it from a brokerage report, or is it from a coffee break with Sam from Shipping? When it comes to your investments—which are about your dreams—always consider the source.

Within an asset allocation and investment context, every person seems to have a different definition of what it means to be conservative, moderate, or aggressive. Your approach can be influenced by several factors. How do you handle volatility and losses? How much confidence do you have in your abilities and knowledge when it comes to financial markets? What am I trying to accomplish and what are you willing to do to get there? How conservative, moderate, or aggressive your investment mentality is will not only inform your asset class choices, but will also influence whether you seek to *exceed* (or would be satisfied *copying*) the investment performance of the index representing a specific asset class.

It also pays to recognize how intensely you think about investing. How tightly do you grasp the steering wheel while driving? How closely do you scrutinize the bill in a restaurant? Some investors are very hands on, whereas others are fairly detached. Do you like to drill down, or do you prefer to focus on the high points? How detail-oriented you are tends to influence the frequency and forms of your portfolio analysis, and whether and how you carry out a performance evaluation. We all need a strategic view, but each of us will approach the tactical rebalancing action according to who we are.

Uncle Frank Says . . .

Be realistic when considering your own investment strengths and weaknesses.

Chapter Seven

Mix, Don't Match

~

In Asset Allocation, Plaids DO Go with Stripes

WHAT GOES UP MUST COME DOWN. This is a law of mathematics, statistics, and even physics. Applied to a set of numbers, the word *mean* is a fancy term for *average*. *Reversion* means "a reversal or return." So, *mean reversion* simply means that through time, something goes back to its average. As applied to investments, the concept of mean reversion or reversion to the mean says that over a period of several investment cycles, most assets' returns will tend to generate their long-term average returns. For example, when Japanese equities' returns in the mid- to late-1980s were far above their long-term average, at some point it became increasingly likely that they would revert to their mean returns by producing returns that were near, or even far below, their long-term average. This is just what happened from 1989 until early 2003. In the 1990s the U.S. stock market, particularly technology stocks, returned *far more* than average. For the first part of the new century, they reverted to the mean and through the mean and returned *far less* than the long-term average. High-quality bonds underperformed in the last years of the 1990s but then became a high-returning investment in the 2000–2004 period.

Uncle Frank Says . . .

Pay attention to the numbers. The numbers don't lie.

Almost every time an asset class goes too far in one direction, it eventually swings the other way—the only questions are how far and for how long. Among the most difficult things to know about mean reversion are how long it will take for above-average returns to fall back to or below their long-term averages, or for below-average returns to increase to or above their long-term averages.

Financial history confirms the difficulty of determining *the persistence of returns* versus *the reversal of returns*. Just because an asset class has been outperforming the average does not mean there is some fixed timetable for prices to drop and then recover or the other way around. Just ask anyone who was short tech stocks during their meteoric rise, or long Japanese stocks during their prolonged downturn. Keep in mind that when the reversing move does occur, prices will often push far past their long-term average in the opposite direction. In Wall Street parlance, *reversion to the moon* means that returns keep on surpassing to the upside while *reversion to the moan* is used when talking about returns staying lower far longer than expected.

Let's take a quick look at how reversion to the mean can help you keep your portfolio in line with your goals and, more importantly, keep you out of trouble. One of the key measures I use to track equities is the proportion of an individual industry group as a percentage of the S&P 500. This is a fairly simple tool that gives me an indication when a group seems to have grown too far or have shrunk too much. Take technology stocks in the 1990s. In 1995, tech stocks composed just about 10 percent of the S&P. By 1999, tech stocks had grown to a whopping 28 percent before topping out at well over 30 percent in early 2000. Without making any judgments about the individual stocks, one could see that the group as a whole had grown far beyond its average weighting and was more than ready to revert back to the mean. If you had followed this measure and decided to cut back your allocation to the group, you would have saved yourself considerable pain. At the same time, energy had fallen from its average 9 to 10 percent level down to just 5 percent. An investor paying attention to mean reversion would have considered switching from tech to energy stocks. With no further economic or financial analysis, just being aware of this concept would have led you to do exactly the right thing for your portfolio. As another example of mean reversion protecting you, by late 2006 financial stocks had grown to 21 percent of the S&P 500, up from below 10 percent several years earlier. Investors who noted this might have considered cutting back financials in their portfolio. As we now know, that would have been exactly the right thing to do based on what happened to financial stocks in 2007 and then into 2008.

Risk is one of those four-letter words that has more definitions than grammatical uses. There are many types of risk, so what are we talking about, exactly, when we discuss risk? Investing, not unlike life, presents each of us with a wide range of risks. There is *purchasing power risk,* which is the loss of value due to inflation. There is *price risk.* Prices change daily for many assets and not always in the direction we would like. *Interest rate risk* represents the impact of interest rate changes on our fixed income assets.

Credit risk is the risk we take that a company in which we invest cannot repay what it owes us. Assets can be revalued or devalued, currencies fluctuate against each other, markets rise and fall, and the economy is subject to fluctuation and change. We need to always be aware of what risks we are facing and what risks we are taking.

In investing, there are two basic ways to approach risk. One is to be risk-seeking and select investments that have higher historic volatility in the hopes of earning higher returns. The other is to be risk averse, completely avoiding investments that have any chance of loss. Each of these postures has a significant impact on portfolio returns. The old adage "no risk, no return," is truest of all in the financial markets.

Returns are what it's all about. The whole point of asset allocation and investing is to protect your capital and earn a satisfactory rate of return. Your return may come from dividends and interest, or it could be a result of long-term gains in asset values, such as the appreciation of stocks or real estate. Some returns from asset classes are fixed in amount, while others are less predictable and are market dependent.

Estimating future returns for asset classes is a blend of art and science, past and present. Most asset class return projections start by taking into consideration the actual total returns generated over the most recent 1-, 3-, 5-, 10-, and

20-year time periods. There are different ways of projecting returns for different asset classes. For equity asset classes, projected returns are based on forecasts of real earnings growth, the expected inflation rate, changes in the price-earnings ratio, and the dividends anticipated over a given holding period. For fixed income asset classes, the variables used to calculate returns include current interest rates and inflation rates, the credit strength of the issuer, and expected changes in interest rates and inflation.

One of the most frequently used concepts in the process of asset allocation is the notion of standard deviation. Web sites refer to it and financial advisors will show you an investment's standard deviation, so you should definitely know what it is. In driving terms, *standard deviation* is a relatively straightforward way of measuring how far your car tends to steer to the right and to the left of the centerline of the highway. In financial terms, we calculate the average return of an asset over a specified time period. Then we measure how far away and how often the returns have been above or below the average. This calculation will give us an idea of how volatile an asset is, and how far away from the average it has swung. Often this can help us determine when a specific asset class might be about to revert to its mean.

In statistical terms, we know something pretty important about figuring standard deviation. Let's take the case of Real Estate Investment Trusts at the end of 2006. The index of REIT shares had an average 10-year return of 14 percent with a standard deviation of 17 percent. We know from statistics that 68 percent of the time you can expect that REITs will range in returns from 31 percent (14 percent + 17 percent) to −3 percent a year (14 percent − 17 percent). When we look at the 2006 return of 31 percent, we see that we were well outside the range of normal returns (14 percent), and thus we probably want to look at lightening our portfolio's exposure to this group. On rare occasions, we may experience an annual return of 2 standard deviations away from the mean or average return. This only happens about 5 percent of the time, according to statistical probabilities. So if, for example, we look at the S&P 500 and see that the 10-year average return is 8.5 percent with a standard deviation of 19.1 percent, we should expect returns to range from −10.6 percent to +27.6 percent about 95 percent of the time. If we see in the newspapers that the stock market is down 25 percent for the year, we know that we are near one of these rare 2 standard deviation events, and we would probably want to be a buyer of the market. This tool works on less volatile assets as well. At the end of 2006, Treasury Inflation Protected Securities (TIPS) had an annual return of 6.2 percent with a standard deviation of 4.5 percent. Looking at the 2006 calendar-year return of just 0.4 percent gave you a pretty good indication that TIPS returns might be about to rise, and you should consider shifting some of your portfolio's assets into that area. You do not have to know how to calculate the standard deviation of an asset class. You just have to know how to use it. Your financial advisors or your other sources of financial advice should be able to provide you with historical standard deviation numbers for various asset classes.

In an asset allocation and investing context, we often look at the relationship between assets. We want to know if a specific asset behaves the same way as another in response to the same economic conditions. People care greatly about *correlations,* because the benefits of asset allocation depend to a significant degree on our ability to find asset classes with correlations of returns that are stable and low (or negative, if possible). What we do not want is a portfolio of investments that behave exactly alike. In a lot of ways, proper asset allocation is the search for assets that are *not* correlated with one another.

Uncle Frank Says . . .

Some of your investments should zig while others zag.

Mathematically speaking, correlation values range between $+1.0$ and -1.0. A correlation reading of $+1.0$ indicates that the assets behave exactly alike. A correlation reading of -1.0 indicates they act nothing alike and respond differently to a given event. A correlation reading of zero indicates that there is no measurable relationship between the two assets.

So how can we use this tool to manage our assets? Let's say you have 30 years to retirement and have decided to put together a growth-oriented portfolio. You want exposure to long-term advancement and growth over that time span. You will want to own some stocks, but you also want assets that can grow and do not act like stocks. They should respond differently to the same economic and financial circumstances. We find that Real Estate Investment Trusts have a historical average annual return of 14 percent and a correlation of just 0.1 with stocks, so you want to consider adding them to your portfolio. Gold has a historical annual return of just 5 percent, but you know it tends to do well in times of high inflation, has a negative correlation with stocks, and thus should do well when stocks do not. Let's add some gold to the portfolio to take advantage of the fact that gold tends to zig when stocks zag. Latin American and Asian stocks usually tend to have a slight positive correlation with U.S. stocks, so we may want to consider them for a portion of your portfolio. We want to use correlation to put together a portfolio of assets that match your objectives, but which do not act alike all the time. This should give you the returns you need to reach your objectives, but dampens volatility to the point that you can sleep at night knowing that you have a balance of uncorrelated assets in your portfolio.

Just as you need to eat a balanced diet with a variety of food groups to stay healthy, you need to allocate your assets to several different kinds of investments to properly manage portfolio risk. Diversifying your investment exposure can be accomplished by having a sufficient number of assets that respond differently to different kinds of economic, interest rate, political, currency, and inflation conditions, among other forces, thus producing returns that are uncorrelated with one another and standard deviation patterns that, in combination, reduce overall portfolio volatility. Although fairly little agreement exists about the most appropriate number of asset classes to have in a portfolio, it can safely be said that six asset classes are more diversified than three asset classes, which are more diversified than one asset class, but 15 or 16 asset classes probably do not offer much more diversification benefit than 10 or 12 asset classes. Because of the increased time demands involved in effectively monitoring and managing a portfolio of more than 10 or 15 asset classes, it is fair to say that it is possible in some cases for a portfolio to be too diversified.

Uncle Frank Says . . .

You want your portfolio to have some assets that have low or even negative correlations of returns with conventional asset classes such as stocks and bonds.

What's the key to proper portfolio diversification? Correlation. You want to own a portfolio that is truly diversified, rather than a bunch of stuff that actually is highly related. For instance, if you have two large-cap stock funds, a value fund and an international fund, you may not be all that diversified. These asset types usually have a positive correlation with each other. Maybe your fixed income portfolio contains municipal bonds, U.S Treasuries, and an international bond fund. Diversified? Probably not as much as you think, since they will all generally respond in similar ways to market events and interest rate movements. The economy has become more global, and it is not enough any more to just add an international component to be diversified. In this case, you might want to consider adding some REITS, real assets, and convertible bonds for diversification.

One of the most important, and yet underappreciated, aspects of asset allocation and investing relates to the role that compounding plays in building wealth. In its most elemental form, compounding involves allowing wealth to accumulate over time. The Swiss have a saying which can be applied to compounding: "For the rolling snowball to get big, the hill has to be long and the snow has to be deep." Another important feature of compounding involves the longevity and the latter years of the overall holding period. For example, for an asset that compounds at an annual rate of 8 percent for 20 years, 41 percent of the *total gain* is earned in the final five years (the final 25 percent) of the holding period.

Whereas *compounding* describes allowing your assets to grow over a certain time horizon without withdrawing any (or too much) capital, *reinvestment* refers to the act of plowing back dividend or interest payments into the original investment in order to earn whatever rate of return can be generated. For sufficiently long time periods, reinvestment can play a major role in the buildup of investment capital. For example, if you hold a $1,000 bond for 30 years until it is paid at maturity, you will also receive the semiannual 5 percent coupon, twice each year (equal to $100 per year), producing a total of $100 $\times$ 30 years or $3,000 in coupon payments. For you to actually earn 10 percent over the 30-year life of this bond by the way bonds work, it is assumed that you will invest each of the two $50 coupons every year at a 10 percent effective annual yield. The same reinvestment principle applies to the reinvestment of dividends back into common stock investments. From 1926 to 2006, if you (or your grandparents) had invested $1.00 in the S&P 500 and reinvested the dividends, your investment would have grown to $3,036.51. If, however, you had taken those dividends and squandered them on high living, you would have just $109.89. Reinvestment is a significant component of long-term returns for most equity and fixed income asset classes.

Using some of the tools to calculate ratios and compile an asset allocation plan requires an advanced knowledge of mathematics. Not everyone has that. Fortunately, today there are many software and Internet services that can supply you with the end result of the calculations. What is important is that you understand the measures and how you can use them to help you put together a successful asset allocation plan.

Uncle Frank Says . . .

Trees don't grow to the sky, and the sky will not fall, but you can take the fruits of compounding to the bank.

Chapter Eight

Our Minds, Our Selves

*Do Not Be Your Own
Worst Enemy*

ONE OF MY CLIENTS DECIDED to invest a large sum of money in one single stock to establish a trust that would benefit her children; the terms of the trust were that it could not be opened or changed for 21 years. After we purchased the many, many shares of the stock at $18 per share, she frantically called me several days later saying, "David, the stock is $17 7/8 per share!" The point of this story is that this investor vowed to think long term, but she couldn't make herself keep her vow.

The single biggest factor in achieving success with an investment plan is not the markets or the economy. They matter, but not nearly as much as *understanding ourselves*. We have to face up to our own mindset and emotions to be successful. Human beings have degrees of built-in biases and feelings about money, risk, and even control. If we recognize this up front and are honest with ourselves about our own thoughts, we are more likely to minimize mistakes. Understanding our own emotions and psychology also allows us to take advantage of other peoples' emotional mistakes by buying when they get depressed and selling when they are ecstatic. Buy Low, Sell High, in other words.

Our mind is a many-splendored thing. It interprets things in different ways at different times. Sometimes, even at the same time. On certain occasions, we are amazingly perceptive. At other times, we miss the obvious. Some days, we can see the big picture clearly and understand the important things. Other days, we cannot think our way out of a paper bag. Sometimes we are contrary and are contrarian in our thoughts. At other times, we find ourselves running with the crowd without really understanding exactly why we are doing so. Economists are generally pretty rational people who rely heavily on numbers and math to understand and explain how the economy and markets function. It may not occur to them that pure math can be distorted by psychology. Irrationally, they assume that investors always act on a rational basis.

In the last two decades of the twentieth century, a group of very bright people began to question this concept. How, they asked, if our emotions and psyche play into every other facet of our lives, from relationships to what we order for lunch on any given day, could we become perfectly rational when it comes to matters of finance? They conducted a lot of interesting and ingenious experiments and came to what now appears to be a sensible conclusion. We couldn't. Our thoughts, feelings, likes, and dislikes influence our finances as much as any other part of our lives. These bright men and women created a whole new school of thought called *behavioral finance*. They discovered that humans are prone to pursue certain incorrect methods of approaching the markets. They found that we often process information incorrectly. We fail to learn from experience. We look for mental shortcuts to avoid doing the work needed to succeed. Any of these factors can cause us to make the wrong choices at the wrong time when we approach our finances and asset allocation plans.

Let's take a look at some of the tendencies that researchers have uncovered. If we are aware of where the land mines are in our thought processes, perhaps we can avoid them. Emotions and psychology are powerful things. If we can make them work for us instead of against us, the probability of reaching our goals soars.

One of the first, and most dangerous, pitfalls we all suffer from in varying degrees is *overconfidence*. We think we are better at something than we actually are. We are all from Lake Wobegon where as Garrison Keillor says, "All the women are strong, all the men are good looking, and all the children above average." The best example of this is the phenomenon of confusing a bull market for brains. I knew quite a few people in the late 1990s who quit their jobs as teachers, executives, or salespeople to become day traders. A few of them sold their businesses to ride the Internet boom. They all considered themselves stock market geniuses riding Cisco, Microsoft, Amazon, and Yahoo to tremendous gains. When you are up 100 percent a year, it becomes easy to think you are the greatest investor since George Soros or Warren Buffett. The self-styled wizards got cocky and stayed in way after the party ended. Not only did they subsequently have to look for jobs in a troubled economy, they lost their gains and, in many cases, their nest eggs and had to start all over again. We need to know what we are good at and what we are not good at it. At all times, we must avoid confusing luck for skill. It's okay to get lucky. Just don't assume that a lucky gain can be repeated because you are so smart.

Uncle Frank Says . . .

Dogma may have been a good movie, but dogmatic is a bad way to approach the markets.

Another huge mistake we make is to be *inflexible and dogmatic* in our approach to markets and to life. We all have what I call an Aunt Matilda. This classy lady is a wonderful woman, knits us sweaters and afghans for our birthdays, and shows up with fudge and cookies every holiday. She is also very fixed in her thinking and refuses to change. As far is she is concerned, Little Johnny is immature and poorly behaved. Never mind the fact that Little Johnny is 45, married with two honor student children, and is a successful executive. Aunt Matilda refuses to change her mind no matter what evidence is presented to the contrary. We need to remain open to new thoughts and new ideas.

Nowhere is this type of dogmatic and inflexible thinking more prevalent than in the financial markets (except perhaps in politics). I have met literally hundreds of investors whose fixed thinking caused them to miss opportunities. They will not read anything that presents an alternative viewpoint or consider any opinion or thought but their own. If they like technology stocks, they only read articles and listen to commentators that favor tech stocks. They dismiss anyone who thinks tech stocks are overvalued. The reverse is also true. I encounter plenty of investors who have a natural curmudgeonly bearish bias and are pretty well convinced that the world will be ending by 5 o'clock today and if not then, certainly, by tomorrow at the latest. They refuse to consider that capitalism, human endeavor, and ingenuity also have a good chance of prevailing, as in the past. They miss the tremendous opportunities that can come from participating in a growing, innovative world. We have to stay open-minded. Different assets will be in favor at different times. In some years, tech stocks will shine. In others, it will be financial stocks, or commodities. The whole point of asset allocation is to position ourselves to benefit from these changing cycles in the world and in the markets.

We need to be aware of what the behavioral finance types call *framing*. Framing is simply how we look at our investments. When we get a phone call about an investment idea involving some new wonderful sizzle-boom-bang investment (and Wall Street comes up with these new sensations with some frequency), do we get caught up in the excitement without considering how it affects our overall investment plan? Do we ask ourselves if it fits in as part of our overall plan to achieve our goals? It is critical to keep the bigger picture in mind when we think about investing and judge each new idea within the context of our long-term goals. Don't buy investments the way you might buy clothes. It's one thing if that magenta shirt looks silly in three months; it's quite another to be saddled with a faddish stock or bond.

Uncle Frank Says . . .

What do you know and how well do you know it?

We need to be realistic in our approach to investing. Just because we want a specific asset to do well doesn't mean it will. We all have a tendency to exaggerate the probabilities that our ideas will be winners. It's entirely human. We do the same in all areas of our life. We convince ourselves that our candidate will win the election or our team will win the Super Bowl. Just ask Super Bowl 2007 Patriots fans which team they were convinced would win in Arizona.

On the other hand, certain people tend to overestimate the risks of investment. We can spend way too much time obsessing about the short-term risk of an investment, particularly those with which we are not that familiar. We place too much emphasis on short-term market movements and do not keep the bigger picture in mind. Our asset allocation plan should be designed to help short-term squiggles work for us, and we have to avoid overestimating the risks as much as we need to avoid underestimating them.

For some people, familiarity may breed contempt, but I find more often in investing that *unfamiliarity creates fear.* Asset allocation works because it forces us to create a portfolio that is composed of diversified and unrelated assets based on specific goals and objectives. By planning for our retirement or to have the money to take that trip around the world for our 30th wedding anniversary, we need to have a mixture of investments that will hopefully gain us the best upside while subjecting us to the lowest downside risk. To accomplish this, we will likely have to put assets in our portfolio that may be new to us and with which we are not very familiar. If we avoid investments in real assets or certain types of commodities and hedge funds because we aren't familiar with them, we may well fail to reach our overriding goals. We need to avoid the impulse to stick with what we are used to, as this may be a serious hindrance to getting us where we want to go.

Researchers have also found that we tend to hang our hat on the wrong information. When we review our investments, we worry about the fact that a specific stock is selling for less than we paid for it, or we take profits simply because an investment has reached a new high price. We make decisions based on arbitrary factors. A given investment does not know what we paid for it. We need to evaluate anew the prospects and potential of each investment and, most importantly, ask how it now fits within our overall plan. If an investment has reached new highs but is still within its historical range, why would we sell it when there is likely still room for upside? If an investment has lost value against what we paid for it, but could still depreciate further over a time period when we will need the cash, the initial loss should not prevent us from selling. Better to have a small loss and the cash we need than a bigger loss and no cash when our child's college tuition comes due.

We also tend to worry entirely too much about the possibility of loss. In 1988 and 1989, one of my clients became concerned that the stock market crash of 1987 was going to happen again and made a fearful, dogmatic decision to go 100 percent into cash and wait for the cataclysm, totally missing out on the rise in the S&P 500 Index from 243 at the end of 1987 to over 1,500 by early 2000. We seem to be hard wired to avoid feelings of loss. Experiments have shown that people will step over dollar bills in the street to avoid dropping a dime out of their pocket. We also tend to resist change even if it is profitable change. Our aversion to loss and to change can make our approach far too hidebound and careful, and consequently we miss the opportunities right in front of us.

One of the mistakes that researchers have found to be all too common is overemphasizing the short term. We let today's news dominate our thinking and forget all about our long-term plan. Next thing you know, we are chasing the market, usually from far behind in the pack. Commodities went up yesterday, so we buy commodities today. Health care stocks went down, so we sell health care stocks. We let television shows and newspapers, magazines, or web sites manage our portfolio in a scattered way, paying attention to some news and ignoring, or not even being aware of or understanding, other news and events. This is the most arbitrary way you could possibly manage your portfolio and is exactly the opposite of sound asset allocation. From a long-term perspective, we want reversion to the mean to work for us as we manage our portfolio. This means paying attention to short-term events without letting them dominate our thinking. We need to focus on the big picture while being mindful of important emerging and changing trends.

Another natural human tendency is to join the crowd. Most of us are social creatures. We like being with others; it's comfortable and often fun to be part of a crowd—for example, at sporting events. But in markets, the herd instinct can quickly get us trampled. It may be comforting to own the same investments that everyone else owns. If everyone we know owns Real Estate Investment Trusts, we may feel more comfortable about buying them. If everyone seems to be selling gold, we wonder if we should get out, too. What does everyone else know that we don't? Follow the crowd, and you'll find yourself buying high and selling low.

We also have individual biases about how we deal with information. Some of us make our choices based on far too little information. We take eight weeks to buy a new necktie or dress, but then make investment decisions that affect our entire life and net worth after an eight-minute phone conversation. We spend three months researching a new car or refrigerator, but radically alter our asset allocation based on a conversation over lunch. Some people get confused by the information flow. Without even trying, we are bombarded from all sides with information. Even if you don't read newspapers or magazines, view a web site, or watch television and listen to the radio, information will still infiltrate your world—in the office, at the health club, at the coffee shop. It is easy to become so overwhelmed that we default to spreading our money equally among all the choices presented to us. Conversely, the information flow can cause us to freeze and do nothing. Sometimes it helps to remember that we aren't so much managing a portfolio, but aiming toward our goals, dreams, and objectives. We need to be methodical and always keep our ultimate goals in mind.

Uncle Frank Says . . .

If you invest out of fear, you will be too conservative
and will never reach your goals.

We all have biases and psychological quirks. The
important thing is, to the greatest degree possible, to be
aware of them and make them work for us. We need to
know ourselves. Ask those close to you (your spouse, your
partners, and your closest friends) or better yet, ask
your Uncle Frank, for an honest assessment of what they
perceive to be your strengths and weaknesses. When
I look at my long-term asset allocation plan and then turn
to my Uncle Frank, he reminds me that I tend to be too
conservative and own too many Treasury Securities and
Treasury Inflation-Protected Securities (TIPS), and I tend
to allocate too much to cash. Uncle Frank forces me to
ask if this approach is really going to achieve my goals and
help me reach my objectives. We must try to be aware of
the cycles of depression and euphoria that have always
been present and always will be a part of financial markets.
Be aware that although going along with the crowd can be
very comfortable and even work well at times, crowds tend
to be wrong at the critical asset market turning points. If
we are scared, we should probably take a deep breath and

reassess the potential positive outcomes. If we are overly excited about a particular investment, we should consider having a nice cup of chamomile tea and ponder the risks.

Be methodical and careful in your approach. Do your homework. Keep the short-term news in perspective and focus on the big picture. Know your weaknesses as well as your strengths. When you hear about a new idea that sounds exciting, ask how it fits in with *your* plan. Your plan is not the same as your neighbor's, your broker's, or your relative's. By focusing on your goals and your objectives and avoiding the highs and lows of your emotions, you can structure and manage your asset allocation plan to take advantage of others' emotions and mental mistakes instead of them getting richer because of yours.

Uncle Frank Says . . .

Did you buy that stock for your plan or for your ego?

Chapter Nine

The Jockey Matters as Much as the Horse

*Pick the Right Rider to Guide
your Portfolio Down
the Backstretch*

ON A PLANE TRIP RECENTLY, I met a voluble fellow and we were conversing about a wide range of topics from securities markets to Maryland seafood. In the course of our talk, it came up that he occasionally likes to go to the racetrack. Not often, and he doesn't bet a lot, but he takes annual trips to Lexington, Kentucky, for the Bluegrass Stakes and enjoys an occasional wager. I asked him how he handicapped horses, and he told me he had a few formulas he liked to use. "But I will tell you, David," he said, "If Edgar Prado was riding on a farm nag against Seabiscuit, I would probably bet on him." In his eyes, Prado was such a good jockey that he could overcome many of the other attributes of the horses in the race. He has ridden and won in all sorts of weather, big races, claiming races, fast tracks, slow tracks, and even on grass. Investing is like that as well. The asset class is the horse we have in the race, but we need to make sure we have the best jockey to increase the likelihood that we do well no matter what the conditions.

Just as some track conditions do not give any advantage to a specific jockey, some asset classes such as government bonds, large-cap stocks, and cash investments are usually efficient. There is a continual flow of information, and everyone has pretty much the same information on which to base their decisions. Any advantage gained from the jockey is relatively small. Most of the reward comes from the horse itself. The jockey is more or less along for the ride and to make sure the horse doesn't decide to take a nap in the backstretch or go off track. On the other hand, once you begin to consider investing in less efficient, less well-researched asset classes, it becomes imperative that you devote time, effort, and resources to identifying good, rather than average, jockeys.

Some asset classes such as small-cap equities, emerging markets, and high yield bonds require a jockey who knows the track and can race under a wide range of track conditions. Others, such as hedge funds and managed futures, are the asset allocation version of Edgar Prado on a farm nag. It is *all* about the manager. For still other asset classes, such as real estate and private equity, you need a local jockey who knows the track. He has to have specialized knowledge of a particular industry group or the location where investors are buying and selling. My own research shows that the difference between an average jockey and a great one in these asset classes can be as much as 5 to 20 percent a year! Under difficult and challenging track conditions, your choice of jockey makes a much bigger difference than it would on clear, dry days with perfect conditions.

Uncle Frank Says . . .

Who is riding the horse and on what kind of track are they running?

It is possible to have exactly the right asset class and have your returns ruined by choosing the wrong manager.

If you go to the track and see that the world's fastest horse is running in the sixth race at Keeneland and David Darst is the jockey, do not bet on the horse! It may well be the right horse, but you definitely have the wrong jockey. At its essence, investment manager selection is all about judging human beings. Whether you do it yourself or use an advisor to seek out the best for you, you will be evaluating how well they know the track and how they have performed under different kinds of conditions in the past.

In a lot of asset classes, manager selection often boils down to a choice between *passive investing,* where you are just trying to replicate that particular asset's makeup and returns, or *active investing,* where the goal is to do as well as or maybe a little better than the asset class as a whole. Passive investing can be fairly easily carried out through index funds, which charge very low investment management fees. In addition, numerous exchange-traded funds (ETFs) have been created as convenient, easily tradeable ways to mimic the investment performance of asset classes, subasset classes, and even industry sectors.

Active investing also offers several choices. You can use regular open-end mutual funds that buy and sell shares at the end of every business day. There are numerous closed-end funds as well. These funds trade on the various stock exchanges instead of directly accepting and redeeming funds themselves. Because they are fixed pools of money, they do not have to worry about investor redemptions, and they frequently can invest in less liquid assets than can regular open-end mutual funds.

The flow of information about asset managers tends to vary in detail, timeliness, coverage, and objectivity according to the type of investment being considered. Some of the independent resources available are offered free of charge or at minimum cost, while others charge subscription- or demand-based fees. For index funds, ETFs, and open-end and closed-end mutual funds, you can find basic information about past investment performance and sometimes evaluation ratings of investment results online and/or in the printed versions of such sources as *Forbes* (www.forbes.com), *Barron's* (www.barrons.com), *BusinessWeek* (www.businessweek.com), The *Wall Street Journal* (www.wsj.com), and *Investor's Business Daily* (www.investors.com). More detailed information on funds, including specific fund holdings, can be found via dedicated sources such as Lipper (lipperweb.com), Morningstar (www.morningstar.com), or more broad-based information providers such as Bloomberg (www.bloomberg.com), Thomson Reuters (www.thomsonreuters.com), and FactSet (www.factset.com). The proprietary web sites of practically all the asset management companies usually contain background information about

their own organization and their roster of available investment choices.

For alternative investments such as hedge funds and
funds of funds, you can locate varying degrees of detail
on the web sites of Hedge Fund Research (www
.hedgefundresearch.com), CS Tremont (www.hedgeindex
.com) Hennessee (www.hennesseegroup.com), and other
dedicated providers. Managed futures fund information
can be found through Barclay Commodity Trading
Advisors (www.barclaygrp.com). A limited degree of partnership information about managers in asset classes such
as real estate, oil and gas interests, timber interests, private equity, and venture capital can be accessed through
Cambridge Associates (www.cambridgeassociates.com).

Finding out about the managers in various asset classes
takes some effort. Not everyone has the time or the
resources to accomplish this. You have to be willing to do
quite a bit of research, sometimes seeking out creative
ways to dig deep into the financial media and even government filings by the various managers. You will need to be
able to pull together a wide range of information to form a
clear, concise picture of who the manager is and how he or
she performs under different track conditions. And please
know that many times when locating and evaluating managers, you are competing against battle-tested, full-time

professionals fortified by a vast network of contacts and organizational memory.

Uncle Frank Says . . .

Do you know how long your money manager has been doing the job well?

It takes some effort to select the best asset managers for your portfolio and objectives. Given this, an important decision is whether to do the research yourself or use the resources of a professional to assist you. You may have a particular market or asset class where you have specialized knowledge. As a result, you want to select managers yourself in that category and rely on a professional in the areas where you lack expertise. If your plan calls for some of the less efficient or less liquid asset classes such as hedge funds or private equity, you may well decide you need a consultant to select the right manager.

Whichever course you choose, there are some basic yet important questions that you will want to get answered to help you assess and select investment managers. Exhibit 9.1 lists 10 key questions to use in evaluating and selecting asset managers.

EXHIBIT 9.1   Ten Basic Questions for Evaluating and Selecting Investment Managers

1. **Ethics:** Can you provide a written statement of your professional experience and code of ethics?

2. **Philosophy and Approach:** What are the key tenets of your investment philosophy and approach?

3. **Investment Edge:** From what sources do you derive your special investment insight, investment expertise, and investment edge?

4. **Disciplines and Tools:** What disciplines and other tools do you employ in determining when to buy, hold, or sell an investment?

5. **Human Capital:** How do you attract, hire, train, evaluate, and motivate your professional and support staff?

6. **Performance History:** Can you provide details about your absolute and relative results and the persistence, consistency, and variability under varying market conditions of your returns, standard deviations of returns, and correlations of returns with other asset classes?

7. **Lessons Learned:** How do you apply your view of the world and lessons from previous investment mistakes to anticipate and protect your portfolios against the major categories of risk exposure you face?

8. **Costs:** Can you provide detailed information about the costs, turnover, and tax efficiency of your asset management services?

9. **Capture Ratios:** When your asset class has experienced rising prices, what percentage of the upside have you generally been able to capture (the "Upside Capture Ratio"), and when your asset class has experienced failing prices, what percentage of the decline have you generally suffered (the "Downside Capture Ratio")?

10. **Capabilities:** What is the most important thing that I've neglected to ask about your investment management that you want to make sure that I know and understand?

Not all the information you need is going to be available in written materials such as marketing literature and prospectuses. Some of this information will need to be obtained by direct communication, whether it is a phone call, e-mail, or even an in-person meeting. Many of the questions in Exhibit 9.1 refer to information that generally can be discovered from the investment manager's written marketing materials or web site. If you are unable to get good answers to the questions in the checklist, or to other questions of importance to you, you might want to look for other managers and consider finding additional assistance in finding the right manager.

Given the significant amount of time and in-depth knowledge needed to find a money manager, many people decide to use an advisor who specializes in the selection process. If you elect to go this route, you need to satisfy yourself that you are choosing a thoughtful, diligent, and trustworthy advisor who knows what he or she is talking about. This not only means that they possess good judgment and insight but it also implies that they recognize and stick to operating within their circle of knowledge and competence. In short, they know what they know and they don't pretend expertise in areas they don't know.

It is highly likely that the information you need to select an advisor will come from personal meetings and a

EXHIBIT 9.2   Five Basic Questions for Evaluating and Selecting Manager-Selectors

1. *Criteria:* Which quantitative and qualitative criteria do you consider most and least important in evaluating and selecting investment managers?

2. *Process:* What are the specific processes you use to find, approve, monitor, and terminate investment managers, and can you supply details concerning the identity, frequency, and reasoning behind your decision to fire investment managers?

3. *Experiences:* Can you furnish insights from particularly positive and particularly negative manager selection experiences about investment manager attributes that are (1) analyzable and relatively easy to find out; (2) analyzable and relatively difficult to find out; and (3) unanalyzable but extremely important?

4. *Success Factors:* What evidence can you supply concerning the likelihood of your being able to select first-quartile (A-Student) investment managers?

5. *Value Added:* What are your distinctive competencies in manager selection and how do you translate these skills into value added for your stakeholders (clients, employees, and owners)?

---

review of the advisor's written material. Exhibit 9.2 contains a list of five basic questions to use in evaluating the people who will select a manager for you.

In addition to the five areas of inquiry described in Exhibit 9.2, if you are considering hiring an advisor to help find a manager, you should also seek information concerning some of the factors listed in Exhibit 9.1 concerning ethics, sources, philosophy and approach, human capital, performance history, lessons learned, and costs.

Selecting investment managers and advisors boils down to evaluating people. For this, you need perceptiveness, wisdom, patience, emotional intelligence, and a sixth instinctual sense to tell you when something doesn't feel right. In the immortal words of the late Paul Cabot, Treasurer of Harvard University and one of the most successful asset allocators of the twentieth century: "You not only have to get the facts, you have to face the facts." If something seems off or you are not entirely comfortable, dig deeper. If you cannot resolve the reasons for your hesitation, you might need to seek out a different jockey for your horse.

One of the most important criteria by which to judge a potential investment manager or advisor is transparency. Are the manager's investment processes, investment decisions, investment positions, and investment successes and failures fairly easy to see and evaluate? Some information will be proprietary, and there are some things that cannot be disclosed for regulatory reasons. Nonetheless, it is critical that you or your advisor have the right level of understanding about what the investment manager is doing with his or her business, and you need to develop a level of confidence that the people who have a right to know and a need to know, *do know* what is going on.

One item in Exhibit 9.1 mentions capture ratios. This ratio tells us how our jockey does in good track conditions.

This is good to know. What is considered a decent capture ratio tends to vary by the magnitude and duration of the asset class upturn or downturn. We want to know that the jockey rides well and wins when the track is dry. We also want to look at how he does when the skies open up and the track is muddy. Can your manager ride in mud and do well when the asset class is generally out of favor? You will want to look at his or her average up and down returns, which groups all the positive returns together and averages them, and combines all the zero and negative returns together and averages them. You will also want to review best and worst period returns, which look at the best and worst returns for various time periods. How long does it take the manager to recover from a loss? How often does he win? How often does she lose compared to the other jockeys in the race? Does he or she return more or less than the benchmark for their asset class over time?

In some asset classes, it is possible for a manager to be among the best for long periods of time. We call this *persistence of performance*. For other asset classes, it is extremely difficult for an asset manager to repeat investment success over long periods of time. That's why it's important to try to find out whether the investment manager's processes and idea flow will work under different market and economic conditions. Although none of the following signals guarantee persistence of returns, there are some indications that they may point to improved chances of doing so. We want to look at things like employee turnover. If the people are constantly changing, so is the quality of ideas and information. Does the manager's firm have a strong culture with ingrained traditions and methods that can be expected to continue? Are they passionate about their work? A brilliant man or woman who does not care is average at best. Do they respect and monitor the risks of their particular asset class?

In everything we do in life, our success and/or failure can depend on what we choose not to do as much as what we choose to do. Manager selection is no different. If we are able to get our money back from, or better yet avoid investing money with, ineffective, reckless, or fraudulent investment managers, we can save time, money, anguish, and opportunity cost (which is the equivalent of firing managers before engaging them). Adapting the Hippocratic Oath taken by medical doctors, "First, do no harm," to an investment manager selection context, we might say, "First, stay away from bad money managers so they can do no harm to you."

One of the most frequent indications of poor investment performance is a dysfunctional and disruptive work environment within an investment organization. Uncontrolled egos, lack of teamwork, jealousy, disloyalty, backbiting, and other symptoms of internal conflict usually undermine the firm's ability to function.

Another valid reason to terminate investment managers is when you observe them drifting away from or jettisoning altogether the process and methods you hired them to use. If your small-cap stock manager starts buying shares of IBM, it's time to consider changing jockeys.

When you find that your investment manager intentionally or unintentionally takes on risks with your capital that you had not bargained for, that's also a good reason to part company. These risks may include a wide variety of financially perilous behavior. If, for example, the manager you select to manage your government bond portfolios starts buying complex and volatile mortgage securities, or your blue chip equity conservative money manager starts using margin, it is time to reevaluate and consider finding a new manager who will stick to what you hired him to do.

Selecting the right jockeys to ride your stable of horses is critical to the success of your long-range plans. Whether you want to just match the returns of a specific asset class, or outperform it over the long run, you will want to have the right jockey on each horse. Monitor your managers' performance closely, perhaps even closer than you monitor your asset allocation mix. It is essential to make sure that your portfolio has a good day at the track and that it is working to make your dreams a reality.

Uncle Frank Says . . .

Sometimes you should change jockeys midstream.

Chapter Ten

Riding Out Storms

~

Be Prepared for the Inevitable

THE WORD *PROTECTION* COMES FROM the Latin *pro* meaning "in front of" and *tegere,* meaning "to cover." For many investors, portfolio protection refers to the range of asset allocation strategies, investment instruments, and mentalities that we can use to defend all or a portion of our assets against loss. Psychology and good old fear and greed are what drive us to protect ourselves against loss. Not only is it important to understand your personal psychological makeup, but you also need to be aware of naturally occurring fluctuations in your (and others') level

EXHIBIT 10.1   Cycles of Investor Interest in Portfolio Protection

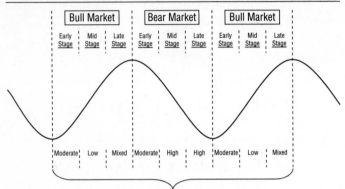

Degree of Investor Interest in Portfolio Protection

of fear and greed based on market cycles. Exhibit 10.1 illustrates how fear and greed can wax and wane with market highs and lows.

During the early and mid stages of a bull market, investor interest in portfolio protection ranges from moderate to low. As the bull market ages and moves into its more advanced, mature, and perhaps speculative state, investor interest in portfolio protection tends to become more defined by investor personality and self-awareness. Cautious investors begin to look for ways to protect the gains they have achieved in the rising market. Less cautious, less self-aware investors tend to adopt the "What? Me worry?" approach of *Mad* magazine's Alfred E. Neuman.

As asset prices top out and begin to move downward, risk moves to the forefront. The cautiously wise investor maintains and perhaps adds to his or her protection. Overly optimistic and aggressive investors hope that the selloff is only temporary and that prices will return to new highs. When the bear market of falling asset prices picks up momentum in its mid stages, more and more investors begin to think about and search for various kinds of portfolio protection. In the late stages of a bear market, interest in portfolio protection remains quite high, reflecting elevated levels of investor frustration, disenchantment, disillusion, and despair.

Uncle Frank Says . . .

Always be aware of what phase of the market cycle you are in right now.

In recent years, increasing numbers of strategies have been developed to help investors protect their portfolios. Over the years, the idea of protecting portfolios has evolved from diversification alone to asset allocation.

Before exploring some main avenues of portfolio protection, it is wise to keep a couple of things in mind. First, some of the best, yet most often overlooked means of portfolio protection involve having an appropriate degree of diversification. Second, a written statement of investment objectives can act as a focal point during volatile periods to keep us from tossing out the baby with the bathwater. Lastly, when in doubt, see your Uncle Frank. He will give you perspective—into the markets and yourself.

Recall that one of the main points of asset allocation is the search for noncorrelated assets. One of the most straightforward means to achieve portfolio protection is to have exposure to mainstream asset classes that will thrive during unfavorable market conditions. This means that you should consider different assets such as gold or inflation-protected securities that usually do well in highly inflationary conditions. You might want to include asset classes like food and pharmaceutical stocks that tend to hold up well during recessionary periods and can deliver reliable dividends. To protect against serious geopolitical upheaval, you might want to own certain types of managed futures funds as part of your overall portfolio. To be a successful asset allocator, you want always to have some assets that preserve their value when the investment world seems to be coming unhinged. In the words of the British poet Rudyard Kipling, "You want to keep your head when all about you are losing theirs." Some of the asset classes that have tended to exhibit consistently low correlations of returns with other asset classes include domestic and nondomestic cash instruments; managed futures; precious metals; commodities; oil, gas, and timber interests; and inflation-indexed securities.

As Wall Street legend Daniel Drew proclaimed, "He who sells what isn't his'n, must buy it back or go to prison." The same holds true in the stock market. In the stock market, you can profit from falling prices by borrowing shares of a stock from your broker and selling them. If you are correct and the price falls, you simply buy them back and return the shares to the broker. The greater the price drop, the more profitable the short sale. Of course, if it rises, you might have to buy the shares back at higher prices and lose money. Investors have traditionally been able to access short-selling through hedge funds that have focused totally or in large part on this investment strategy. However, beginning in 2005 and 2006, a number of mutual funds and exchange-traded funds were introduced to *sell short* various broad asset class indexes or specific asset class subsectors. Some of the funds have been structured to deliver a multiple (such as twice) of the positive or negative returns of a conventional short-selling fund. Unlike the unlimited loss potential involved with the outright shorting of asset classes or instruments, short funds have limited risk since the investor's maximum loss is confined to the amount of the investment. As a result, short-selling mutual funds and exchange-traded funds may be allowed in Individual Retirement Accounts (IRAs), whereas outright short-selling activity is not. Check with your tax advisor.

Uncle Frank Says . . .

You can protect yourself, but make sure you know the cost.

One of the more important and least understood risks is the need to protect against a falling domestic currency. Don't forget: We live in a global economy and our portfolio should reflect the way the world is, not the way we might wish it to be. Currencies can have a dramatic impact on the international part of your portfolio. In the best case, the nondomestic asset that you purchase *goes up* in price, and the nondomestic currency in which it is denominated also *appreciates* against your home currency. In the worst case, the nondomestic asset that you purchase *goes down* in price, and the nondomestic currency in which it is denominated *depreciates* against your home currency. Until recently, small to mid-size investors could not afford the costs associated with protecting against unfavorable currency movements. Thanks to the introduction of currency exchange-traded funds, it has become possible to gain relatively liquid, inexpensive currency exposure by other means than through the traditional institutionally-dominated cash and derivative foreign currency markets. For the first time, you can diversify from your home currency at a reasonable cost without large amounts of leverage.

A *derivative* is an instrument whose price movements are driven by, or derived from, the price movements of some underlying asset, such as a stock index, a bond index, or a group of commodities. Options, futures, forwards, and swaps differ from each other as to whether and when you have the *right* or the *obligation* to buy or sell the underlying asset. There are also different ways to price various kinds of derivatives as well as a daunting range of amounts and types of margin or collateral that must be posted. In their most basic form, derivatives of all types are employed in search of portfolio protection by entering into a position to protect against adverse movements in the underlying assets. For example, to protect against falling stock prices, you might sell short stock index futures. You might also consider buying a stock index put, which is an option to sell the underlying index at a fixed price. It will gain in price if prices fall. For the most part, derivatives trading is best left to specialists—and specialists whom you trust. Investors looking for exposure to these instruments may do well to avoid the do-it-yourself approach in favor of a hedge fund or a managed futures fund that specializes in them.

Even though many forms of portfolio protection do not involve outright visible costs, sometimes there are hidden costs such as the loss of purchasing power or missed opportunities because of money tied up in low-return protective investments. Insurance costs money. Psychologically, it's not uncommon to feel like it's worth the cost if something bad happens and the insurance kicks in to cover the loss. However, if the skies remain blue and the insurance isn't needed, we tend to wonder if we are paying too much for it. And maybe we are. You may miss the upward price move of an asset class because you've placed too much emphasis on protecting your investment from the downside potential. Of course, many of the strategies for portfolio protection do involve outright costs such as commissions or hedge fund manager fees. It is critical that you know what the outright and the hidden costs are of any type of portfolio protection strategy you may use.

Protecting your portfolio is like any other kind of insurance. How much coverage do you want? How high a deductible are you prepared to have? What is the value of what you are insuring? The higher the value of the asset and the lower the deductible, the more the protection will cost. Do you want a rider to increase coverage on a particularly valuable piece of jewelry or an antique? That costs more. The more you cover, the more it costs.

Protecting your portfolio works exactly the same way. Do you want to protect just one asset class of your portfolio or the whole thing? Generally speaking, the greater the degree of coverage, and the more complex the protection arrangements, the more it is going to cost you.

Other considerations enter into the picture as you attempt to protect more and more of your portfolio. Let's assume that after talking with your advisors, drinks with Uncle Frank, and careful consideration, you come to the conclusion that under conditions of extreme financial duress for your conventional portfolio (causing prices to drop an average of 30 percent), some of your portfolio protection would increase in value by 40 percent. Exhibit 10.2 shows that having various percentages of portfolio protection asset classes or strategies will dampen the degree of portfolio losses that would have occurred otherwise if 100 percent of the portfolio had been invested in conventional asset classes.

If 50 percent of the portfolio had been invested in portfolio protection asset classes (or investment strategies), the overall portfolio outcome would have been +5 percent rather than –30 percent (Circle A in Exhibit 10.2); if 30 percent of the portfolio had been invested in portfolio protection, the overall portfolio outcome would have been –9 percent rather than –30 percent (Circle B in Exhibit 10.2); and if just 10 percent of the portfolio had been invested in portfolio protection, the overall portfolio

EXHIBIT 10.2   Protecting Your Portfolio

Ratio of Conventional vs. Portfolio Protection Asset Classes	% Decline in Conventional Assets	% Increase in Portfolio Protection Assets	Overall Portfolio Result:
	−20%	+5% +40%	−5% +10%
50%–50%	−30%	+10% +40%	−10% +5% Ⓐ
	−40%	+10% +40%	−15% 0%
	−20%	+10% +40%	−11% −2%
70%–30%	−30%	+10% +40%	−18% −9% Ⓑ
	−40%	+10% +40%	−25% −16%
	−20%	+10% +40%	−17% −14%
90%–10%	−30%	+10% +40%	−26% −23% Ⓒ
	−40%	+10% +40%	−35% −32%

outcome would have been −23 percent rather than −30 percent (Circle C in Exhibit 10.2). Exhibit 10.2 also shows overall portfolio outcomes for other price declines for conventional asset classes (−20 percent and −40 percent) and for other price increases besides +40 percent (+10 percent) for portfolio protection asset classes.

How much or how little of your portfolio you allocate to portfolio protection will be influenced by your objectives and goals, your investment outlook, what assets you own, and your personal financial situation at any given time. Can you suffer losses and, if so, how much? What are your financial needs and when do you need funds? Know yourself, know your needs.

Uncle Frank Says . . .

Always ask yourself: "How bad can it get?"

Chapter Eleven

Build Your House on These Rocks

―⁓―

The Stronger the Foundation, the Better the House

IN ALL AREAS OF LIFE there are certain must-haves. If you are flying to San Francisco, you must have a ticket. If you are taking a long car trip, you must have a GPS or a road map. If you are making rockfish with black bean salsa, then you need rockfish filets and black beans. If you are fielding a baseball team, you must have nine players as well as bats and gloves. You get the idea. To accomplish any task from the mundane to the sublime, there will be certain things you must have. So it stands to reason that there are certain must-haves to implement a successful asset allocation plan. These are concepts and guidelines to get you to your goals or dreams. As the world changes around us and we are living longer under uncertain health care and social security conditions, the must-haves become more crucial.

As you move through life, get an education, and develop the skills that will help you succeed in your career, you become the owner of a critical asset, your *human capital*. This is your lifetime earnings potential. How much of this human capital you will be able to turn into *financial capital* depends on several things. How much you earn, how much you spend, your lifestyle choices, and how you plan for and deal with taxes and inflation will all affect how much human capital you will be able to turn into financial capital over time.

Thoughtful consideration of human capital can help you decide how much risk to assume and what kinds of assets to emphasize at various stages of your life. Exhibit 11.1 shows the shifting proportions of a typical individual's human capital and financial capital during his or her lifetime.

It is important to keep in mind that each of us is different and the path for converting our human capital into financial capital will not be as smooth as the lines in Exhibit

EXHIBIT 11.1   Human Capital and Financial Capital over an Investor's Working Lifetime

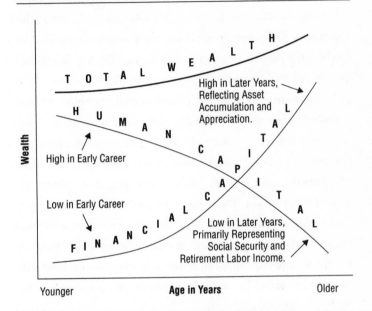

11.1. How we live our lives and the choices we make, as well as fluctuations in financial markets and economic conditions, will have an impact on the human capital to financial capital conversion process. How we choose to earn our living will have an impact as well. The human capital line for a Wall Street trader will have more fluctuations than for a professor with a regular salary and retirement plan contributions even if the trader ends up with more (or less) financial capital in the end.

For most of us, human capital will act more like bonds, with regular steady conversion from human capital to financial capital. For a few risk-taking individuals, the flow will be more stocklike, with jumps and setbacks in the process. Most of the time as we allocate the newly converted capital, we will want to emphasize equity and growth assets in the early and middle stages of our earning years and as we age, we begin to shift toward income-producing assets. As we get closer to retirement, the amount of annual additions to human capital will tend to decrease, and we will likely begin to use our financial capital to replace the reduced income from earnings. Remembering to include your human capital within the context of your investment universe is as important as taking account of all your other asset exposures, and will also be affected by your investment circumstances and your investment outlook.

Your asset allocation plans need to be a part of your overall financial architecture. There are certain must-haves as you construct your financial house. Do you have a financial plan? I am always amazed at the number of people who do not have any idea of how much they will need to retire or even have some concept of their monthly budget. I see successful entrepreneurs and young people just starting their careers with the same lack of insight. How can you even begin to devise an asset allocation plan if you don't know where you are? Uncle Frank would say it's impossible.

Is your human capital protected? Do you have adequate life insurance to replace your income to protect your family in the event of an unfortunate event? Are your real assets such as your home, car, and other possessions adequately insured against loss? A little thought and time spent organizing your personal finances forms the foundation of your asset allocation strategy.

Uncle Frank Says . . .

You have great worth. Now put it to work to make money beyond your current income.

Everyone should have and periodically revise a financial plan. If you do not have one, you need to put one together now. It doesn't have to be perfect. You may not want to sit down and think about your income and expenses and what the purpose of your investing is meant to be, but you have to. With all the tools available at the click of a mouse today, it is fairly easy to put together a comprehensive plan to accomplish your goals. It is simply a matter of deciding what your dreams are, discovering what resources are available to achieve them, and what steps you need to take to get there. If you are not the do-it-yourself type, there are many financial planning firms and advisors who can assist you. Just compare and monitor the costs and fees associated with these services. Make sure the person you select does not have his or her own agenda and is not primarily driven by selling you certain financial products.

Boiled down to its essential features, financial planning involves gathering information about your current circumstances. You will need to make reasonable projections about your income, expenses, capital inflows and outflows, savings, taxes, and investing returns. You will want to consider personal matters such as the size of your family and the cost of the education you want for your children. How and where do you want to retire, and what charitable gifts are important to you? You need to develop possible scenarios and detours that may occur along your journey. You will also need to review and revise your plan from time to time. I would suggest a thorough review at least annually.

Taxes will undoubtedly play a part in your investment and financial plans. Taxes have an impact on what types of investments we all choose and how we own those assets. Tax laws grow more complex every day at the state, local, and federal levels. They change frequently. This is an area where you will most certainly want to obtain quality professional help.

Trusts and estates represent a special part of the tax code involving transferring assets to the control of trustees to accomplish some special goal. A trust can also be used to protect, manage, or transfer and distribute assets under certain circumstances. Frequently they are used to help plan the transfer of assets after death in the manner we wish, and to plan for estate taxes. This is another area where I strongly suggest you avoid the do-it-yourself impulse. Trust and estate structures are extraordinarily complex and hard to establish and manage without specialized skills and knowledge.

Another important and frequently misunderstood area of your financial architecture is life insurance and annuities. In short, life insurance tends to be purchased to protect human capital against death by providing money to help pay estate taxes and/or replace our human capital for our loved ones. Annuities are generally purchased to protect against living a long life, since they pay a stream of fixed or variable payments that have been initially funded through a large lump-sum purchase or through a series of regular payments.

Many kinds of life insurance and annuities are available with customizable attributes relating to cost and payment methods. Financial planners who are objective in their approach can help you navigate through the vast array of life insurance and annuity offerings. Other forms of insurance coverage that are worth researching include disability, long-term care, and health insurance. Seek appropriate guidance. It can be worth its weight in gold if it prevents you from using the wrong insurance products for the wrong reasons.

Uncle Frank Says . . .

You must take the time to think about where you are and where you want to go.

When the foundation of our financial house is in place, and we use our asset allocation and investment plans to build and furnish the house, we have to be diligent to keep things in order. Along with regular housecleaning, we have to do periodic reviews. Just as a house needs maintenance and inspections, a review of your asset allocation plan is another must-have. In recent years, a new concept has developed that has proved to be an enormous help in keeping our plans on track.

The whole idea of *lifecycle investing* has evolved out of three concepts. The first is that people's investment goals, risk tolerances, and their preference for capital growth versus capital preservation tend to change as they progress through life. A commonly held notion maintains that aggressive portfolios with an emphasis on equities and growth-oriented investments are more appropriate for younger investors with longer time horizons, and conservative portfolios with an emphasis on income-producing investments are appropriate for more mature investors who tend to have lower risk tolerance.

The second idea is that we cannot base our asset allocation on age alone. The size of our portfolio and short-term needs can have an impact on our plan. A 35-year-old who would usually be focusing on growth assets will probably rethink that allocation for the entirety of her portfolio if she is buying a house in two years. Younger investors saving up for a large expense such as college tuition or a dream vacation may want to be far more conservative than is called for purely by age, and older investors with more than enough assets to take care of their annual expenses may decide to be far more aggressive than usually dictated by age, particularly if their goal is to grow their wealth for their heirs or charitable foundation giving.

The third important concept relates to being aware of future liabilities as well as the future income and expenses that we expect. Retirement, living expenses, health care, and future gifts are all potential liabilities that can have an impact on how we invest today.

Uncle Frank Says . . .

Age is just a number.

When you review your plan, keep these considerations in mind. Although it is generally true that the younger we are, the more we should focus on growth assets and shift toward income as our human capital is converted to financial capital, we also need to be aware of special circumstances that might require a shift in our asset allocation mix.

Another important concept to keep in mind as we monitor our asset allocation plan is what the academics call *portfolio optimization*. This is simply the idea that we want to mix our assets in a way that produces the best possible return for a given level of risk, or stated another way, that assumes the least possible amount of risk for a given level of return. Such portfolios lie on the so-called efficient frontier, which sounds very Star Trek, and is shown in Exhibit 11.2.

Several methods have been developed to help structure assets into efficient portfolios. Some of these methods rely heavily on mathematical techniques, and some are more dependent on rules of thumb or an investor's instincts and judgment. Which one you use is going to depend on your

EXHIBIT 11.2   A Representative Efficient Frontier Curve

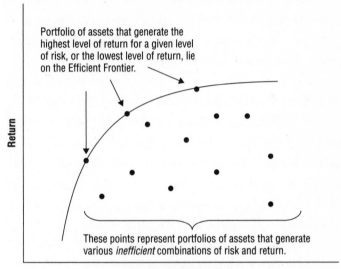

Portfolio of assets that generate the highest level of return for a given level of risk, or the lowest level of return, lie on the Efficient Frontier.

These points represent portfolios of assets that generate various *inefficient* combinations of risk and return.

Return

Risk (Standard Deviation)

personality, computer skills, and comfort level with the math involved.

Wall Street rocket scientists (otherwise known as quants or financial engineers) have developed sophisticated models and programs to optimize portfolios. These strategies used to be the realm of the most sophisticated. Now, there are web sites where you can run Monte Carlo simulations on model portfolios and take them for a test drive.

The whole point of the efficient frontier is to gauge whether your asset allocation is earning you the highest possible return for the level of risk you are assuming. If your portfolio's return and risk parameters lead it to lie *below* the efficient frontier curve, then you may need to tweak the asset mix to see whether the portfolio's risk is as high as it could be in view of the portfolio's risk level.

In addition, most financial planning firms use these tools to keep your asset allocation mix in line with your goals and the efficient frontier of asset allocation. There are several of these asset allocation models available, and they can all help you maintain the right mix. Some web sites worth exploring include effisols.com, allocationmaster .com, ibbotson.com, and vestek.com, as well as the web sites of many of the leading securities brokers and mutual fund management firms.

Portfolio management is similar to home repair. Years ago, our parents could fix the relatively simple furnace or ceiling fan. Today, much of the equipment in our homes is now run by a computer chip or miles of wires, and it is not as easy. Sophisticated diagnostic equipment and specialized skills are needed. It works the same way in portfolio management. When asset allocation was just stocks and bonds, with maybe a few international stocks, rebalancing and managing the asset mix was a fairly straightforward, back-of-the-envelope analysis. As the range of asset classes has expanded and the amount of information has burgeoned, we need a bit more power to see the full picture. Powerful tools such as Monte Carlo simulation can help us manage our portfolios to better achieve our goals. It is not really necessary that we understand the complex math behind them; we just need to know how to harness the results to monitor and manage our assets.

Computer power is awesome, but don't forget the intuitive tools. The age-based and goal-based approaches to keep our allocations in line are also valid. But keep in mind that, even the most powerful computer program cannot capture how we feel.

Uncle Frank Says . . .

In life, computers are right 95 percent of the time when things are normal, but may err the other 5 percent of the time when things are abnormal. That's when you need human beings.

Count to Zen

❧

Use the Numbers to Calm Your Mind

ZEN IS A SCHOOL OF BUDDHISM that emphasizes practice and experimental wisdom to attain awakening. The word *zen* derives from the Sanskrit term "dhyana," a specific type or aspect of meditation. Zen focuses on the acceptance of the present moment and yourself as you really are. It uses meditation to help you focus on what is important right now. These are useful traits in managing your investment plan.

Investment success is attainable, but is not guaranteed no matter how well-conceived the asset allocation plan. As in many aspects of life, the odds of your achieving wisdom and success can be enhanced through practical thought and reflection. Along the way to achieving your goals, you need to pay attention to certain guidelines and principles intended to shape and sharpen your efforts.

From the start, *you need to know who you are.* Not who you think you are or who you want to be, but who you are right now. It is all too easy to think we are someone we are not and such self-delusion can have a drastic impact on our investments. You may think you are more of a risk taker than you actually are and end up panicking and making a bad decision out of unanticipated fear. You might think you are a better investor than you really are, and think that your investment gains were from brains, not luck. This could easily cause you to reach too far and make mistakes that result in damaging losses.

Knowing yourself and coming to terms with such knowledge represent difficult but highly worthwhile goals. Warren Buffett has repeatedly advised investors to find and develop their own circle of competence and stay within it. Are you more comfortable with certain assets (without limiting your options, of course)? Are you a hands-on investor who prefers to own real estate to provide growth, rather than stocks or Real Estate Investment Trusts? Do you like to uncover and research investment ideas yourself, or are you more comfortable relying on others? What resources and how much time do you have to do the research and cross-check your conclusions? How important are your goals and dreams?

Another area to give some careful thought to is your investment activity and results. How often and how carefully do you review and track your portfolio? Are you able to explain the causes of your investment gains and losses? What styles of investment approach do you prefer? Do you have a preference for growth stocks or for value stocks? Are you comfortable with a hedge fund, or are you more comfortable with the more transparent and liquid mutual funds? Are you subject to any positive or negative investment biases that you hear about?

Knowing yourself is an ongoing process. You need to compare your own impressions of yourself with those that others have of you, especially Uncle Frank. Without knowing who you are and how you might react to various situations, you *might* find investment nirvana. But it will be an accident, not a calculated result.

What can you genuinely know, and by what means can you discern it? Humans may have five physical senses, but our survival and well-being hinge also on our sixth, seventh, and eighth senses—our intuition, our instincts, and our feelings. Eons of evolution have trained our brains to process enormous amounts of information and filter it all down to what is essential for our continuation of life.

Asset markets may change, technology may change, financial conditions may change, and trading mechanisms and structures may change, yet human beings' response patterns have tended to remain constant through the ages. If something in the investment world doesn't feel right, pause, conduct further analysis, and check additional sources. If it still doesn't quite add up, let it pass. It is not wise to allocate assets and invest based purely on instinct, and it is equally unwise to ignore your gut instincts when doing so.

You need to recognize your asset allocation and investment mistakes, learn from them, remember them, and avoid repeating them. Over time, you want to learn when to change your mind and follow a different path. This could be for any number of reasons: The markets have become too risky, your original outlook has proved correct, or your projections were off-kilter. Put another way, you need to develop flexibility and adaptive behavior.

One of the most important aspects of the whole process is analyzing the reasons why an investment turned out badly or turned out well. Did you shoot from the hip and not do enough research? Did you rely on faulty sources? Were your fundamental assumptions wrong? Was the investment outcome successful, but for the wrong reasons? Was the reasoning sound, but the timing too early or too late?

Uncle Frank Says . . .

It is not really a mistake if you learn from it.

A successful asset allocation and investment feedback cycle involves gathering sufficient information and evaluating it. Once you have done this, you have to make your investment decision. You should have a clear, concise idea of why the specific investment does or does not perform as you anticipated. Regardless of how it turned out, what did you learn from this particular investment decision?

The other side of the flexibility coin is focus and conviction. There is a difference between holding firm to your principles and being pigheaded. The problem is knowing what the difference is and when it matters. Markets will move against you over the years. Should you add to the position or is it time to rethink your original assumptions and get out? Did you miss a critical factor that can cause disastrous results? It is difficult to come up with the right answer, and you can't do so without challenging your original decision and looking for flaws in your reasoning. It may well be that your original conclusion was right and you should add to your position, but you need to know what you might have overlooked or just been plain wrong about.

Some of the greatest asset allocation and investment success stories have been made possible by keeping a sense of perspective and seeing the big picture. Think about an investor in the late 1980s who could have foreseen the tremendous impact of the personal computer. How about an investor who had recognized when Internet stocks had gone too far? An investor who recognized the implications that a capitalistic China would have for the rest of the world in the first decade of the new century would have realized substantial profits. The ability to spot big picture societal and market trends can have positive results for your investments. Sometimes you will feel the wind at your back, and other times a gale will blow in your face. If you know which way the wind is blowing, you can position yourself accordingly. Trends can be driven by political change, scientific or technological breakthroughs, or changes in tax laws or monetary policy. The ability to recognize them when they occur can be critical to your success.

The key is being able to recognize when trends are emerging and how sustainable they are. You need to understand what segments of the economy a given trend will be positive for, and where the fallout will be negative. The person who realized the implications of the Model T would have benefited enormously by buying the new auto stocks and selling all her shares in the buggy whip companies. You need to identify investable themes and determine which asset classes and specific investments will benefit from these trends.

You have to live in the real world. You need to be realistic as you set your goals and determine how long it will take to reach your goals. Apply a good dose of reality when it comes to what sort of returns an asset can provide over a certain period of time. The same holds true when evaluating a particular money manager. A healthy dose of realism and perhaps a touch of skepticism can help prevent dashed expectations and poor outcomes.

One of the most important things to keep in mind is that trees really do not grow to the sky. At some point, all high-growth investments begin to slow and sometimes they crash to earth. Competition arises, demand eases off, and growth begins to decelerate. Keep in mind that it is not different this time. It never is. All trends, no matter how powerful, have an ending phase where the profit potential begins to fade. Phrases such as "New Paradigm" have wreaked incalculable financial damage on investors' portfolios.

In his magnificent poem "The Second Coming," the Nobel Laureate Irish poet William Butler Yeats wrote, "the center cannot hold," a feeling all too often shared by investors when it appears that prices will not stop falling and the end of the world is near. On August 13, 1979, a renowned and highly reputable magazine ran a cover story, "The Death of Equities." At that moment of widespread and seemingly unending financial pain, it was actually time to be buying U.S. equities.

It's always darkest just before dawn. No matter how bad things may seem, the world is not likely to come to an end. You need a degree of cynicism in investing, but you should avoid extreme pessimism and paranoia at the same time you are keeping excessive optimism in check.

Uncle Frank Says . . .

Don't be contrary with your partner but be a little contrary in the markets.

We all need to maintain a stance of healthy contrarianism. *Contrarianism* means being willing to have opinions and positions that are different from the majority. Often when a vast majority believes that a particular investment is either right or wrong, the opposite opinion turns out to be correct. If everyone loves it, there is a good chance you should be selling that particular asset. If everyone hates it, it may well be time to buy.

Although being a contrarian is a useful and sometimes valuable investment approach, like everything else, it is not foolproof. A mass of people running out of a crowded movie theater is not in and of itself a valid reason for you to go running in. Sometimes, the consensus is just plain right. You need to be able to distinguish whether this is the case.

In life and investing, we all make mistakes. What we do after we realize we have made a mistake spells the difference between success and failure in our ongoing plans. It's an entirely human trait to avoid pain, to deny that an investment loss is in the making, and to postpone taking action that will mean the loss becomes a realized loss rather than a paper loss. All too often, not facing up to a problem and admitting our failure will make things much worse as the loss grows ever larger. A losing investment not only affects our results but it can also erode our confidence and cause us to lose focus. Deal with your mistakes up front, be aware that you will make mistakes in investing, and know that you can learn and recover from them. Recognize when it is time to cut your losses, move on, and get over it.

Today more than ever, you have to be selective about which information and educational sources you pay attention to. Ask yourself if the information source is thoughtful and logical, or is it more a short-term source of ridiculous tips that encourages overtrading in riskier assets? Tune out the world's cacophony and avoid distractions. Less is more. Learn which sources are reliable and accurate and ignore the rest.

In the asset allocation and investment realm, using zenlike meditation and focus can help us achieve our goals. We need to pay attention to and be able to evaluate a steady stream of often contradictory themes. Being aware of who we are, what is really going on in the world around us, and how such trends and events influence our investment portfolio will take us a long way down the road to reaching our goals. These factors will help us develop a game plan, follow it, and make the needed adjustments when they are necessary as we and the world around us grow and change.

Uncle Frank Says . . .

Sometimes, buying me a steak dinner is the best investment you can make.

Chapter Thirteen

Seven Quick Ways to Ruin

~

Don't Smother Your Dreams!

Rᴜɪɴᴀᴛɪᴏɴ. ᴛʜᴇʀᴇ ɪꜱ ᴊᴜꜱᴛ no way to make it sound nice, is there? In addition to its connotations of chaos and catastrophe, in the here and now, *ruin* describes disorder, confusion, and any condition that causes torment or misery. In asset allocation and investment decision making, several key mistakes can lead us down a nearly certain path toward investment ruin. In order to help avoid this great unpleasantness, let's take a look at the common mistakes and miscues so we can seek to avoid them.

Being unaware of the risks you are taking is one of the quickest ways to find yourself on the road to perdition. Giving little or no thought to the risks you will face in your investments and overall asset allocation is deadly. You have to consider in realistic terms what can go wrong with every decision and choice you make. During favorable investment conditions, it is especially easy to let your guard down, to ignore risk, to find yourself open to fraud (it is said that more frauds are perpetuated in bull markets than in bear markets since during down times people are naturally more cautious). It is when everything is wonderful and markets seem perfect that you want to consider how to protect your portfolio and keep the gains you have made. Waiting until after the market turns down will often be too late.

Uncle Frank Says . . .

An investment will not always come back in price. In fact, it often goes lower.

Simply being aware of various kinds of risks is not enough. You have to identify the types of risk you are facing and how to protect yourself from them. There are many types of risks you will face on the road to your dreams. There are asset class–specific risks, such as currency movements or perhaps credit downgrades in your corporate or municipal bond positions. There are market-specific risks caused by changes in the underlying economy or by excessive valuations. Investor-specific risks include making sure your asset base is large enough to handle volatility and help you meet your goals. This category of risk also includes the biases and psychological tendencies we have already discussed, such as overconfidence, anchoring, and getting caught up in excessive optimism or pessimism.

Another certain path to disaster is to take comfort in the crowd. We often feel more comfortable in being *wrong with the crowd* than we feel in being *right alone*. If everyone else at the cocktail party last night is losing money in the same stocks and funds you are, you feel more comfortable with your losses. It becomes easier to wrap yourself in the cloak of majority belief that your losing investments will come back, regardless of evidence to the contrary. Rather than always listening to the majority, you sometimes need to stick to the guidelines of your plan and ignore the crowd. They may be right. They may be wrong. But blindly investing with the crowd is like letting a random group of people manage your portfolio and dictate your asset allocation. All too often, by the time an investment is widely owned, it is ready to revert to the mean and go the other way.

You should ask yourself and others, "Is this investment idea or theme a crowded trade?" A call to Uncle Frank is probably a good idea. If it is already popular and widely owned, what are the valid reasons the trend will continue? What are the reasons that could cause it to change direction? Following the crowd may work sometimes, but on balance it will probably lead to subpar returns.

Uncle Frank Says . . .

If everybody is doing it, you very well should not.

Assuming that a good investment will be good forever is usually a sure ticket to despair. It is never a wise idea to assume that just because a particular asset or fund is doing well, it will continue to do so. There is an ecological cycle to most investment classes. Just as a forest grows too crowded with life and growth, leading to the inevitable forest fire, at some point investments and asset classes become too crowded with investors and the profit potential diminishes. It is in the aftermath of the fire, in the fertile dust and ash of a bleak landscape, that new life begins to take hold and reach for the skies. Likewise, a given asset class is probably a better investment after everyone has sold. Remember the concept of reversion to the mean. It is one of the most important tools in your asset allocation toolbox.

Tossing out every investment that falls in value or doesn't perform according to our expectations can also put us in a bad place. Chasing performance alone can have us selling at the very moment we should be buying more. Often, we may be tempted to jettison an asset class or investment manager because they are not keeping up with the torrid pace of a hot sector. That is usually not the right decision. In the late 1990s, a group of thoughtful businesspeople asked my opinion about firing one of the twentieth-century's outstanding value and emerging markets investors from their college investment management roster because his results had not kept pace with the outsize returns that technology stocks had been generating. It would have been exactly the wrong time to let the manager go, and I was able to talk the committee out of their decision. Over the next four years and afterward, this about-to-be fired manager's results were outstanding, both on an absolute basis and relative to the sharply deflating technology sector.

You should ask yourself whether the asset class, investment manager, or investment vehicle has merit. If so, then consider whether its lagging investment performance is likely to improve. Before you rush to make a change, close your eyes and picture the New York Public Library's main building at Fifth Avenue and 42nd Street. New York's popular Mayor Fiorello Henry LaGuardia renamed the two limestone statues of lions Patience and Fortitude. May these leonine sentinels be your constant companions as you monitor your portfolio.

More investors have dug their own way to ruin than seems fair. In mid-2007, *Forbes* magazine reported that a Wharton School Pension Research Council study of 1.2 million individual participants in 1,500 retirement plans found that over a two-year period, 80 percent of the participants made no portfolio adjustments and 11 percent made only one single adjustment. As a result, even those who started out with the right asset mix let the performance of various asset classes determine their overall portfolio strategy. By ignoring the asset allocation mix, and not using an advisor to tell them when and how to rebalance the portfolio, or simply not taking the time to do it themselves, their portfolio was soon no longer structured to their needs. In asset allocation, it pays to face up to whether you are capable of being your own contractor or doing your own home repairs—and if you *are* capable, will you take the time?

Nobody says you have to be an expert at asset allocation and investing, nor do you have to devote all your time and energy to be successful. What you do have to do is choose how involved you are going to be based on your capabilities, talents, and time. Are you going to hire advisors to help with the process? Do you prefer, with the generous assistance of your Uncle Frank, to do it yourself? Whichever choice you make, it is important that you go it alone or hire a professional for the right reasons. Avoid superficial shortcuts or just letting things drift along without paying attention. Either one can have a negative impact and delay or dismantle your dreams.

Another quick path to dashed expectations and returns is to let your emotions rule your decisions. Humans experience a wide range of feelings, but fear and greed are the two most frequently cited emotional forces that drive financial markets. They can rule us and ruin us if we aren't careful. Whereas a certain amount of fear can cause us to be prudent and cautious when we need to be, and a little greed can lead us to take intelligent risks, an excess of either can cause us to veer far off course.

Uncle Frank Says . . .

Fear and greed can be your greatest enemy or your greatest asset.

It is crucially important not to let yourself get carried away by greed. A desire to make as much money as possible right now can lead us to make overly risky investment decisions. It can cause us to set aside our well constructed plans and abandon our principles and become short-sighted and reckless. When we become controlled by greed, we tend to lose touch with the voices of reason and the temperate nature needed to achieve our dreams.

At the other end of the asset allocation and investing emotional spectrum lies fear. Let's be honest. Financial markets can be scary. There can be stomach-churning sell-offs and disruptions. We can freeze at such times if we let our fears dominate us. We begin to see disaster where there is perhaps opportunity. Fear can cause us to abandon our asset allocation plans. It can keep us from shifting from rising assets into falling ones as reason, even though counterintuitive, would dictate. Fear will put us on the road to buying high and selling low. Excessive fear can cause us to make dramatic shifts in our well-thought-out asset allocation and investment plans and abandon good-quality asset classes, investment managers, and investments at exactly the wrong moment.

Fear can also lead you to sit on the sidelines too long, waiting for the perfect investment moment, which never seems to arrive and then suddenly, it has passed you by and you wait even longer for it to return. Unfortunately, it may never return. Another common mistake produced by excessive levels of fear is attempting to time asset class price movements. Several studies have shown that up to

50 percent of many assets' compounded long-term return performance is actually earned during as few as 20 or 30 trading days. If you were waiting for the absolutely most favorable time and missed some or all of this relatively small number of trading days, you missed out on as much as half of the asset's return-generating potential.

It's a big investment world out there, and we need to keep our eyes on the key long-term trends that shape the economy and financial markets. You need to focus on the big picture and not just where the Dow Jones Industrial Average or gold closed on any given day. There are many important forces that affect society, economic life, and asset markets. We need to be aware of them and their impact on our plans. A narrow-minded, short-term focus can cause you to miss seeing these powerful trends and how they affect your long-term asset allocation plan. Although sailing a ship into port does indeed involve a lot of attention to activities that are right in front of you, you must always keep your eye on the horizon for changing winds and potential storms or you will never reach the harbor of your destination.

The whole process of establishing and monitoring an asset allocation plan can be overwhelming. Break the tasks down into manageable pieces and deal with them one at a time. To attempt to sit down in one session to develop a picture of the economy and outlook, set your allocations, and pick asset managers and individual investments is an almost impossible task. Take them one at a time and weave them into a comprehensive plan. Be methodical and thorough. It takes time and a certain amount of effort, but your dreams are worth it. It can appear to be so large a task that you simply do nothing rather than get in over your head. You can prioritize these objectives and decide which ones should be carried out by you and which ones by others.

In a sense, this common mistake—of being so focused on the macro elements of investing that you undermine your effort—is the opposite side of the mistake of taking your eyes off the horizon. If you only look at the horizon, the sails will not be set properly and the rudder will be unattended. Your port, your destiny, and your objectives can never be reached in such a manner.

Chapter Fourteen

The Road Less Traveled that You Should Take Right Now

Your Dreams Are Worth Effort and Attention

AS THE ROBERT FROST POEM so beautifully communicated, you will come to a fork in the road as you move through life. You will be given a choice between the well-trod path or the one less traveled. You can invest as most people do with an assortment of stocks, bonds, and mutual funds bought for various reasons over the years in an uncoordinated fashion. Or, you can take a more holistic approach and view your investments in light of your life and your goals. After all, is there a better reason to invest than to make life be all that you want it to be?

The other side of the coin is that most of us don't have much of a choice in the matter any longer. The risk and responsibility of managing our finances, particularly our retirement finances, have been placed squarely on our shoulders. Gone are defined and guaranteed pensions. Today is all about Roth IRAs and 401(k)s, where we make our own decisions.

The temptation for many, as this brave new world of investing has opened to us (or been thrust upon us), is to focus case-by-case on assets to the exclusion of a thoughtful plan. It is more exciting to think about investing in China (or Brazil, or India, or whatever new emerging market is taking the world by storm). Commodities may have been booming of late, so we better get some of those. Hedge funds may be all the rage—how do we get them? All of these may (or may not) be perfectly good assets for our portfolio, but they are the ingredients to a great recipe, not the dish itself.

Compared to exciting new investments, asset allocation can seem boring, but the importance of thoughtfully formulating a plan can't be overstated. Studies have shown that 90 percent of the differences in returns for large U.S. pension funds over the years is from differences in their asset allocation. Their performance was ultimately not about which managers they hired or what securities they picked, but what asset mix they had at any given point in time. The performance of some of the most successful endowments, from Harvard to Yale, from Duke to Stanford, from Exeter to the Kamehameha Schools in Hawaii, has been a result of their asset mix and changes made in anticipation or reaction to economic, financial, political, and currency developments.

You have a choice: Go into the markets without any idea of what investments can and can't do for you, buy them on whimsy, and cobble together a portfolio that has no purpose—except vaguely "to make money." This would be like going to the grocery store and buying items without any thought to what you plan to cook or even for what meal you are purchasing the ingredients. Maybe you don't like to shop for food or even to cook. Perhaps you prefer to eat out. Even if you leave the meals to someone else, you at least know whether you want breakfast or dinner and your restaurant options. Approach investing in yourself and your life goals the same way: Decide what you want and learn enough to know what is available. You don't need to become the equivalent of a *New York Times* restaurant critic, but you'll do well to keep up enough to know whether a restaurant is reliable or has been closed five times for health code violations.

Formulating an asset allocation plan will not be the easiest thing you've ever done, particularly if you don't know anything about the markets. You will need to take steps to become an informed, educated investor. You will have to stay on top of news and events that can affect your investments. It may be easier to assemble a portfolio based on suggestions from investment salespeople and advertising, but will that help you achieve your goals? The salesperson and company doing the advertising are probably more worried about their own children's college educations and their own retirement plans than yours. Taking the time to learn enough to either be able to hire the right people to manage your investments or to do it yourself will require some effort on your part. But it will be worth it.

Uncle Frank Says . . .

There is a lot of information out there. Find it, be skeptical, be selective, and use it!

So, how do you get started? What should you do right now? How should you approach the whole process of asset allocation and investing? The best way to tackle any challenge is to break the task into manageable pieces, prioritize them, and knock them off one by one. At its core, successful asset allocation and investing involves understanding, evaluating, and managing people. These people include you, research sources, securities brokers, asset allocators, money managers, and other professionals involved in putting your plan together.

Judging people takes insight and instinct. You will use different criteria when evaluating your tax specialist than you will in picking a money manager since the two specialties obviously require different skills. Regardless, you should have some basic fundamental criteria to apply across the board. In all areas, you want to deal with individuals who are honest, professional, and who have high standards and personal integrity. You want the players on your team to be enthusiastic about their profession and open to learning new ways to approach markets. It will be helpful to review your past successes and failures in judging people and learn from both. If you had to fire someone before, ask yourself why, and ask yourself why that person appealed to you in the first place. If you have a money manager, accountant, advisor, or attorney with whom you are particularly pleased, look at their attributes and articulate what traits they possess that seem to work for you.

One of the easiest things to do in assessing the quality of your potential asset allocation and investment team is to ask for references and check them. I have seen far too many people hesitate to take this critical step. I am not sure if they are too shy, or think it's impolite, but it is a critical mistake. Most financial advisors have references and are happy to supply them. In fact, refusal to provide references is a sign that you may want to reconsider using this person.

When contacting references, I suggest that you reach out to them in person or on the phone rather than by e-mail. As Peter Steiner famously captioned in a *New Yorker* magazine cartoon, "On the Internet, nobody knows you're a dog." Much can be learned from tone of voice and other verbal signals that are simply impossible to capture electronically. A hesitation in answering a particular question can often provide important insight. Be direct and say who you are and why you are calling. A friend's or associate's initial response when you ask for a reference to a professional may also speak volumes. Without reading too much into the exchange, you should attempt to discern the level of genuine satisfaction that the reference has experienced with the source of financial help you are considering.

Uncle Frank Says . . .

You wouldn't hire a babysitter for your children without checking references. Why would you hire someone to watch your money without checking their references?

In drilling down on an advisor's references, among the most important things you want to find out are the best and worst things the reference has encountered in working with the advisor you are evaluating. Are the reference's responses unbiased, realistic, and complete? If you still have questions, concerns, or lingering doubts, ask for more references and check for consistency in the responses. The little extra effort invested into the reference-checking process can help you become a better informed and more empowered consumer in deciding whether to proceed with engaging a financial resource.

Not only as part of the evaluation process, but on a regular basis if you decide to proceed, you should physically visit your asset allocation and investing intermediary's place of business. You can learn a lot about people by the atmosphere, mood, environment, orderliness, and character of the place where they carry out their professional activity.

Is their place of business quiet or bustling with activity? What is the degree of formality or informality? How is the space laid out? Does it feel right to you or do the premises seem dicey? Are they organized and efficient? Do they have the technology and information sources they will need to help you? By what means does information arrive at and circulate within the space? From a series of visits, how much turnover do you notice in the professional and support staff? Do they appear enthusiastic and constructively engaged in their duties?

When you visit the physical premises of your financial services provider, introduce yourself to the person in charge of the office, and get a copy of her business card. Even better, try to learn something about her background, and tell her something about yours. In other words, make a personal connection. If the professional and support staff realize that you are at least acquainted with the office manager and you know how to reach this person, it tends to increase the quality of the relationship between you and the others in the firm. The manager can have an impact on how much money they make and often has a great deal of influence over their career. Knowing that you know the boss usually leads to improved service.

You can meaningfully improve the odds of success in your asset allocation and investment activity by continuing to build your knowledge base and by expanding the universe of your investment options. Always be learning. Warren Buffett once said that one of the keys to becoming a successful investor was to read a lot. Stay current on what's going on in the world. Periodically review the financial advisors you are using. Are they doing what you hired them to do? All too often, investment people can develop a form of financial inertia. Your advisors' approach to the markets and asset allocation process may no longer match yours. Too many investors start out relying on one person for advice on investments, taxes, estate matters, and other issues. As your portfolio grows and your situation changes and becomes more complex, you may well need to expand to more specialized advisors. You may be inappropriately relying on only one person to give advice on asset allocation, investment manager selection, tax advice, and trust and estate planning. Although it is possible for one individual to pull together the resources from within and outside the firm and deliver these services to you, you need to evaluate whether this person is capable of staying up-to-date on the latest thinking in all these fields. If you don't feel that your financial professional is growing and staying current, make your concerns known and ask questions. If reasonable answers are not forthcoming or your affairs are not adjusted to your satisfaction, it may be time to change or expand your choice of advisors.

For many years, gaining exposure to markets such as precious metals, commodities, and currencies was something only the very wealthiest investors could obtain.

Today, thanks to the rapid growth of ETFs, everyone has the ability to access just about all asset classes. Looking for foreign real estate? There are general ETFs for that. Want to buy Swiss currency? There is an ETF for that, too. In general, many of these new funds are less expensive and more liquid than the traditional methods for accessing these asset classes. There has been an expansion of financial products in the last decade that makes developing an asset allocation plan and finding appropriate noncorrelated assets that we want easier than ever before. You may be able to significantly improve the risk-reward profile of your portfolio through exposure to these products. As exciting as this is, if you and your advisors are not staying on top of the changing marketplace and are unaware of what is available, new opportunities will be worthless to you.

Particularly in the less efficient asset classes where good manager selection can make a significant difference in portfolio outcomes, you and your advisors should try to be aware of outstanding investment managers who establish new funds or reopen existing funds that have been closed to new money. Fund-related information is available through a wide variety of sources such as the Internet and mutual fund research services. Your advisors should be on top of these, but the mainstream financial press also covers these comings and goings fairly well. You should already be reading publications such as *Barron's, Forbes, Fortune, BusinessWeek, Investor's Business Daily,* and the *Wall Street Journal,* so keep your eyes open for outstanding new and reopening funds. In today's wonderful world of technology, you can even set up a news search using a search engine such as Yahoo or Google that will instantly and automatically send you news of fund openings and closings.

Most of us read the newspapers and keep up with the arts, sports, fashion, entertainment, world events, and politics. We should do the same for the business world, economics, and our investments. You may never want to pick stocks, but you should be aware if interest rates are headed higher or lower or if business is expanding or contracting. In other words, you want to know as much about the business and market climate as about politics or world events. By not reading a section of the newspaper or ignoring business news, you will be left at a distinct disadvantage. We learn about the real estate market when we go to buy a home, so why wouldn't we learn something, generally, about the market in which we're placing so much of our human and financial capital?

Many of us do not give ourselves enough credit for our own insights and knowledge on the investment and asset allocation process. An incredible amount of information is available today via the Internet, television, and the financial press. Ideas and tools that were previously the personal province of Wall Street and big business are now available on Main Street and right in your own living room. Just by paying attention as you shop, drive to work, and even socialize can provide valuable information about the economic landscape.

A lot of us run our own businesses or have careers that give us terrific insights into the world around us. We know how other companies in our industries are doing. Are our suppliers raising prices or cutting them? Are currency fluctuations hurting or helping your sales and your raw material costs? Are new tax laws having a negative impact on your company's business? Are executives in your field confident or downbeat about the prospects for your industry? All of these insights contain valuable information that can help you manage your asset mix and reach your goals.

If you are an executive or own your own business, odds are that your neighbors may be at the same level in their career as you are. They may well have insights from their own industries or companies that will shed light on economic conditions or trends. You may have a neighbor who is a very successful investor who can provide suggestions about current market conditions. Of course, you always want to do your own homework, but your friends and contacts can be great sources of ideas and practical suggestions. They may have some expertise in an industry or company that takes the air out of your sure-fire investment idea. Another valuable tool can be ideas gleaned from informed individuals with specific knowledge at neighborhood cocktail parties, cookouts, and across the back fence.

Uncle Frank Says . . .

An informed friend is a good friend.

It cannot be said too many times that the amount of information and tools available for investors today is practically unlimited. We do not suffer from a shortage of information. On the contrary, the big question is how to parse what is available and use that which is most beneficial. There is no magic list of the best web sites, blogs, magazines, newspapers, or analytical tools. Today's great source may be replaced tomorrow by something else entirely. What works for me may not work for you.

One of the biggest breakthroughs in financial news has been the Internet. You can use search engines to access a mind-boggling amount of information. I just typed asset allocation into one of the popular search engines and got more than 19 million hits! There are blogs, newsgroups, and chat boards as well as more traditional news and information sources. You need to be careful and confirm the information obtained from many of these, but you will find that the Internet gives you a powerful advantage over your parents and grandparents in reaching your goals. A good basic guide to exploring, navigating, and optimizing your usage of the Internet can be found at www.learnthenet.com.

Believe it or not, Wall Street can be a valuable source of information. Brokerage firms and commercial banks publish never-ending stacks of reports on individual companies, industry groups, and the economic outlook. Many firms provide financial planning and asset allocation worksheets that are very helpful. The Federal Reserve Bank publishes reports that review the current state of the economy. Mutual fund shareholder letters are filed at least semiannually with the Securities and Exchange Commission and may give you insight into the thoughts and views of some of the very best money managers in the business.

An incredible range of information sources is at your disposal. It is up to you to decide which ones you find useful. You will have no trouble finding resources that you trust and can rely on for global insight that will be useful in managing your portfolio. Of course, asking Uncle Frank what he reads is not a bad idea, either.

Mostly, open your eyes and ears to the world around you, take good counsel, and take the time to make a plan.

Who Are You?

Determining Your Investment Profile

1. How old are you?
2. How secure do you feel about the ongoing stream of income from your occupation and your investments?
3. How many years until you hope to retire?
4. What is your life expectancy after retirement?
5. Do you prefer do-it-yourself asset management or would you prefer to hire outside advisors and managers?
6. What is the source of your investment capital?
7. What are your primary investment objectives? What goals are you trying to reach?

8. When do you expect to need money from your portfolio?

9. Are you aware of the potential conflicts between your goals?

10. How much risk or loss can you absorb in your portfolio?

11. Will you be making additional contributions to your portfolio?

12. How confident are you about your income and expense projections?

13. What is your tax status? What changes to your tax status do you anticipate?

14. If you need to make more money to meet your goals, is this a possibility?

15. What is your current net worth?

16. What steps have you taken to protect your assets and earning potential?

What Do You Think?

Determining Your Investment Outlook

1. What are the factors likely to affect the financial markets?
2. How strong are these factors?
3. When and by what means are they likely to have an influence on the global asset markets?
4. What are your investment priorities? Are they long or short term in nature?
5. Are conditions in the global asset markets going to improve or worsen in the near term?
6. How long will these factors have an influence on the markets?

7. How have the markets behaved recently?

8. What could cause the global asset markets to reverse course in the near term?

9. How do recent returns for asset classes compare to historical returns and volatility?

10. Is the economy weakening or strengthening?

11. What is the outlook for inflation and deflation?

12. What are the major risks to your investment plans right now?

13. What are the strongest influences in each asset class right now?

14. What could cause these to change?

What Works for You?

*Determining Your
Investment Selection*

1. How does your desired return compare to your risk profile?
2. Do you prefer growth- or income-oriented investments?
3. How do you feel about foreign investments?
4. Are non-U.S. investments currently acting the same as domestic investments?
5. Are you comfortable with illiquid investments where the potential for high returns is offset by some degree of difficulty in redeeming your investment?
6. Do you understand the risks and rewards of the asset class you are considering?

7. How will adding this asset class affect your overall portfolio?

8. How does the proposed new asset class correlate with the other asset classes currently in the portfolio?

9. What are the general trends for the asset you are considering? How strong are these trends currently?

10. What is likely to reverse the current trend for this asset?

11. Is it easy to buy and sell this asset?

12. What are your choices for buying this asset class?

13. What are the tax consequences?

14. What are the costs and fees associated with finding, monitoring, buying, selling, and owning this asset?

Don't Take My Word for It

———————— ❧ ————————

WHILE I WOULD LIKE TO THINK that over the years I have made a modest contribution to understanding and using the asset allocation approach to portfolio management, my work and ideas don't stand in isolation. Rather, I have stood on the shoulders of giants throughout my career and have turned to others for their inspiration and groundbreaking contributions. I do not expect you to just accept David Darst's word alone that the asset allocation approach to investing your money can be quite beneficial. My analysis and strategy are supported by decades of research, insight, innovation, and wisdom from many great minds.

One of the brightest luminaries who has addressed the subject of asset allocation and investment results is **Charles Ellis.** He has written more than 10 books and countless articles on the benefits of sound investment planning and taking a long-term approach to the financial markets. One of his most important books is the classic *Winning the Loser's Game,* in which he shows how investors let the short-term fluctuations of the markets unduly influence their thinking. He demonstrates how investors can use such fluctuations for their benefit instead of being victims of circumstance. He examines using active versus passive index-based investing for long-term portfolios. He shows individual investors how to use the long-term thinking and asset allocation strategies that he has witnessed and/or developed for some of the world's largest financial institutions and investors during the past 30 years.

Some of the early foundations for using an asset allocation approach to investing were developed by academics. In the July/August 1986 issue of the *Financial Analysts Journal,* **L. Randolph Hood**, **Gary Brinson**, and **Gilbert Beebower** published a critical paper entitled "Determinants of Portfolio Performance." The paper demonstrated that using passive indexing of asset classes performed better than active managers who attempted to pick the right investments and time the market. Even more important, the study concluded that asset class selection rather than active management had the biggest impact on long-term investment returns. A follow-up study was conducted by **Roger Ibbotson** and **Paul Kaplan**. Published in the January/February 2000 issue of *Financial Analysts Journal,* their study "Does Asset Allocation Policy Explain 40, 90, or 100 percent of Performance?" reached some startling conclusions. Comparing 94 balanced mutual funds to an allocation strategy of domestic stocks and bonds as well as foreign stocks and cash, they found that the asset mix of the funds was responsible for 40 percent of the *variation among funds' returns* over time. They also found that asset allocation represented 100 percent of the reason for each fund's *total return* over time. Performance had little to do with what individual securities the managers selected and everything to do with their overall asset mix.

One of the more prolific contributors to asset allocation thinking and practice has been **Peter Bernstein**. He has written nine books on the financial markets and scores of articles. He is the founder of Peter L. Bernstein, Inc., providing economic and investment advice to institutional and individual investors all over the world. One of his more important books, *Capital Ideas,* was published in 1992. In it, Bernstein discusses many of the breakthroughs in economic and investing theory and how they can be applied to manage investments. That book was followed in 2007 with a sequel, *Capital Ideas Evolving.* Bernstein's renowned 1998 work, *Against the Gods,* presents a highly readable and engaging history of risk, and shows investors how to identify and manage risks.

William F. Sharpe is a Stanford University professor whose work on asset pricing models won him the Nobel Prize in 1990. He developed a measurement for evaluating manager risk and reward that has become an industry standard. Virtually all evaluations of mutual fund and hedge fund managers rely on the Sharpe ratio, which shows how much risk a manager takes to generate returns. In addition to his textbook, *Investments,* Sharpe has written countless papers on investing styles, the asset allocation process, and asset pricing. Sharpe's Nobel Prize–winning study of the capital asset pricing model, "Capital Asset Prices: A Theory of Market Equilibrium under Conditions of Risk," has been reprinted in many leading financial journals and is widely available. It is considered the definitive work on asset returns and pricing. Much of the current approach to asset allocation is a result of his work. His latest work, *Investors and Markets,* breaks down his formulas into usable principles to properly manage investment portfolios.

Jack Treynor is another pioneering thinker who has contributed much to investors' understanding of how markets and the asset allocation process work. In addition to his own firm that advises investors on strategy, Treynor is a senior editor at the *Journal of Investment Management,* one of the leading academic journals in the field. He is the author of more than 50 papers on asset pricing, market structure, trading costs, and market psychology, many of which are included in his 2007 book, *Treynor on Institutional Investing*.

An important contributor to the profession and practice of asset allocation is **David Swensen**, Chief Investment Officer of the Yale University endowment. Using innovative and thoughtful asset allocation techniques, he has helped Yale achieve annual returns exceeding 17 percent since 1985. His first book, *Pioneering Portfolio Management*, describes his methods for finding equity-like asset classes having low correlations with the U.S. equity markets, for selecting managers within these asset classes, and for rebalancing portfolios to keep allocations correctly positioned under changing market conditions. His second book, *Unconventional Success*, shows individual investors how to select the right asset classes and use low-cost exchange-traded funds and mutual funds to achieve their objectives. The book advises individual investors on what kinds of mutual funds and asset classes to avoid and why. Swensen also emphasizes the need to rebalance your portfolio on a timely basis and to keep your investment time frame in mind at all times.

Harry Markowitz made his mark on the academic scene in 1952 with his groundbreaking paper, "Portfolio Selection," which appeared in the *Journal of Finance* and established the foundation for many of the concepts of modern portfolio theory in use today. In 1990, Markowitz shared the Nobel Prize in economics with William Sharpe and Merton Miller for their cumulative contributions to the theories of portfolio selection and asset pricing. He was one of the first to point out that portfolio returns depend as much on asset covariance and risk levels as on security selection.

Market strategist and investment manager **Barton Biggs** was among the first on Wall Street to focus on asset allocation as a viable approach to investing. He has used his extraordinary intelligence, wit, global outlook, curiosity, and experience to help investors identify and exploit market inefficiencies for long-term gains. He was also one of the first on mainstream Wall Street to realize the value of asset classes such as emerging markets, real estate investment trusts, commodities, and inflation-protected securities. His book, *Hedgehogging,* is an insightful account of the people, profits, pitfalls, and processes associated with launching and managing a hedge fund.

Martin Leibowitz is one of those rare individuals who has achieved success in both the academic world and the real world of investing. He wrote the classic, *Inside the Yield Book,* and seminal papers exploring topics such as franchise value in equities (which differentiates between a company's *existing businesses* and its prospective *new investments*), yield curve and horizon analysis (which look at the importance of income reinvestment and realized ending values in fixed income investing), applications to bonds, and alternate investments' role and application in asset allocation. Prior to his career at Morgan Stanley, he served for 26 years as Director of Global Equity and Fixed Income Research with Salomon Brothers, and for 9 years as Chairman and Chief Investment Officer at TIAA-CREF. With boundless freshness, creativity, and enthusiasm, he has developed new ideas, shared them with investors, and put them to work in real-world portfolio management across a wide range of asset classes.

Jack Meyer served brilliantly as the Chief Executive Officer of Harvard Management Company for 15 years and used a comprehensive approach to finding and using successful money managers and investment techniques. He employed new asset classes including timber and inflation-indexed securities, new instruments, new risk control approaches, and innovative portfolio manager compensation to help the Harvard University endowment grow at a rate of 14.9 percent compounded annually during his tenure. He used several core asset allocation and investment principles to earn these multiyear returns. Meyer and his team employed arbitrage techniques to exploit different pricings between assets that were essentially similar. He was among the first large endowment managers to embrace and use complex derivatives such as swaps, options, and forwards to manage risk and enhance returns—all part of an asset allocation strategy.

Before Jack Meyer, and perhaps the single individual who even made a future Jack Meyer possible, was **Paul Cabot**—a true investment pioneer, who in his 95 years worked on behalf of investors with zeal and enthusiasm that were unmatched. In 1924, he founded one of the first mutual funds in the United States. He not only changed company research but also vigorously and loudly spoke out against shareholder abuses in the 1920s, advocating reforms of the legal framework affecting securities issuance, securities trading, and investment management. With good reason, Cabot has perhaps become most recognized for his strategic asset allocation success in persuading his fellow trustees to shift the Harvard University endowment decisively toward stocks after he became Harvard's treasurer in 1948, just as an 18-year bull market in equities began to unfold.

Asset allocation is an essential way to manage your portfolio not only to achieve your long-term objectives but also to smooth out the short-term bumps along the way. For several decades, the subject has been developed, applied, enhanced, and proven to work by a growing population of highly talented and successful academics, researchers, portfolio strategists, investment managers, and individual investors. Practitioners have reaped the benefits of asset allocation for years in the global asset markets, achieving above-average returns while assuming less risk than would be experienced with many other investment approaches and methodologies. Fortunately, many of the investing and intellectual giants have been generous in sharing their thoughts, ideas, and methods so that you can apply them for your benefit and profit.

Acknowledgments

———————— ❧ ————————

WITH ADMIRATION, affection, and appreciation, I am deeply grateful to my supportive and inspiring family, friends, siblings, colleagues, and teammates, as well as my many mentors and teachers from every corner of America and all over the world. Their continuing influence is manifold and profound.

This book owes much to the skill, perceptiveness, insight, humor, wisdom, patience, intelligence, character, generosity, trust, illumination, energy, and sensitivity of many superstars and powerhouses, including A.C., P.v.G., K.W., T.M., M.M., L.B., C.M., M.H., E.T., K.J., D.S., C.W., F.D., B.R., R.M., B.L., D.E., M.C., L.H., M.G., J.H., G.G., J.S., W.H., M.N., M.A., M.D., E.C., R.H., M.B., C.H., S.O., D.S., C.M., J.R., L.C., N.P., M.B., R.V., R.S., M.P., J.D., A.J., N.L., D.P., J.P., K.J., T.A., C.G., R.C., L.R., F.C., and U.F. (Uncle Frank).